T0380655

THE SPIRITUAL IMPOVERISHMENT OF WESTERN CIVILIZATION

BY PATRICK MOONEY

AuthorHouse™ UK
1663 Liberty Drive
Bloomington, IN 47403 USA
www.authorhouse.co.uk
UK TFN: 0800 0148641 (Toll Free inside the UK)
UK Local: 02036 956322 (+44 20 3695 6322 from outside the UK)

Because of the dynamic nature of the Internet, any web addresses or links contained in this book may have changed
since publication and may no longer be valid. The views expressed in this work are solely those of the author and do
not necessarily reflect the views of the publisher, and the publisher hereby disclaims any responsibility for them.

Any people depicted in stock imagery provided by Getty Images are models,
and such images are being used for illustrative purposes only.
Certain stock imagery © Getty Images.

This book is printed on acid-free paper.

ISBN: 978-1-6655-8735-8 (sc)
ISBN: 978-1-6655-8734-1 (e)

Print information available on the last page.

Published by AuthorHouse 05/21/2021

authorHOUSE®

THE SPIRITUAL IMPOVERISHMENT OF WESTERN CIVILIZATION

A tug of war exists inside each one of us. We go on searching with an innate passion for something better. Our desires are never satiated. Our sensitivity begs the question: "Is this all there is?" We purchase items to satisfy our uneasiness and existential ennui. As we grow older, we recognise the emptiness and promises which the consumer enterprise has presented to us. As death approaches, we are compelled to surrender. In the end nature haunts us. Without spirituality, we realise we are little more than a sad sack upon a pole. We also must leave the realm of our materiality. We look outside the virtual reality which our perceptions deemed real, and we hear a trumpet blast instead of a whisper.

No matter our conviction, death becomes a pivotal moment in our earthly lives. We may have paid scant attention to our most unresolved problem in life. We may have avoided it at all costs, but in the end it will corner us, leaving us with no strategy of escape. The big cathedrals of Silicon Valley and Wall Street become trite and useless in the little chapel of our loved ones leaving us. Robots cannot cry; robot hands do not touch or comfort us in our greatest moments of life's contingencies. Robots do not give us facecloths to wipe our tears, nor do they ever feel our pain.

The coming of the internet of things cannot be our second singularity unless it is engendered by the spirit of God. We need the kingdom of the human heart more than anything else if this planet is to continue. Our smart technology has become too hell-bent and aggressive in its lust to destroy us. In the meantime, our religious leaders, without a single moral peep of protest, sleep disinterestedly on their satin sheets of comfort. Where is the spiritual dimension to the whole coronavirus pandemic in our present state of pandemonium? Have we become so atheistic and secularised that even in our foxholes, we no longer cry out to God for help? Where has this transcendent force, which we once believed would help and succour us, gone? Why has our perception of a divine reality been aborted from the truth in the serum of our existence? This absence makes us cold and lonely. Even though Freud could be right in the sense that religion is an opium, despite Freud's cynicism, we move deeper into the rabbit hole, and some reality does not leave us alone. We shiver like the autumn leaves.

The natural world communicates and connects its electromagnetic message, which teaches us that life is more than a mechanical process. Our process into the unknown is the same as the process in creating a new earth. Plants and flowers grow better when they are rooted in the rot of the earth. The stench of the dung heap in time becomes the beautiful scent of the wild flowers in the field. Although atheism denies God, still the ineffability of some higher intelligence prevails. Throw it out the front door, and it comes rushing in through the back door. There is an interrelationship, interconnectivity, and interdependency between all subspecies. An enormous consciousness prevails on all levels of our experience. Human living, even though we may not be conscious of it, is a holy and sacred thing. It exists as the one consciousness which runs through all life. To live is to be in God. To live is to exist in eternal consciousness. To live is to be a conjoined consciousness with all that exists. All is the one consciousness. All is contained and enveloped by it. To say nothing of mysticism, it is science itself which teaches us this. Atheism for the sake of profit and money denies this. Atheism has constructed a paradigm that satisfies neither the perspective of our virtual reality nor the possibilities which consciousness offers. When God is absent, this world falls apart.

Though we may not recognise consciousness cohabiting the trees and the cry of the swan on the lake, still we sense the beauty and transcendence which they suggest to us. Often when we are overcome by the pressures of our culture and an economy gone vulture-mad, we find that it is the natural world which gives us a sense of serenity. Our perception of reality seems to be disjointed and disconnected from the overwhelming evidence of some superb, non-local intelligence and presence. Spirituality relates itself with such an unknowable force, working within all that exists on our planet. Unlike organised religion and atheism, the surrender and acceptance of the unknowable is at the very core of the mystical approach to life. Uncertainty and insecurity are part of the very soul of true spirituality. Organised religion and atheism are propelled by a lust for certitude.

We humans are on a higher evolutionary level than the world of our subspecies precisely because we are conscious of ourselves. Other animals are not on the same mind level as us. We have been indoctrinated to think that all different forms of life are inferior and meant to be used and exploited for our own benefit. We forget that all our subhuman expressions of life belong to the same one supreme, all-enveloping, non-local intelligence. Ours is a relationship which is interconnected and interdependent. All life is holy and sacred because it is governed by the one supreme consciousness. The sawing down of majestic hardwood trees in the jungle of the Amazon cries out to heaven just as much as the cries of cattle and sheep in our slaughterhouses. The young pullets cry against their caged existence and their natural desire to scratch and fly; this is as much a sin as denying our children to wander and wonder. Consciousness is not the reserve of the human condition. Consciousness embraces all of reality and envelops all creation according to its own electromagnetic specification. The serenity and peace which subhuman species proclaim in abundance can be found by the human species when, despite our perspective, we hammer it out through our connection to the natural world.

We are the only creatures on earth who are out of tune with our interior essence. Trees know they are trees and dogs know they are dogs, but the atheistic elite who control the rest of us think they are God. Through indoctrination, they have led us to believe that God is dead. Only matter matters according to atheism. Nature itself, however, is much more professional than any dualistic psychiatry on earth. The sophistication of neuroscience and psychiatry fail when they separate body from spirit. Atheists tell us that consciousness ends with natural selection. There is nothing more to our story except for our discovery. The material alone gives us our perspective according to atheism. Our perspective becomes our truth. Our perspective is objective and ascertained through the medium of our senses. If this is so, then why does science tell us that solidity is an illusion? The atom is almost empty. What we think we see is not objective; it is all inside of our own heads. Natural selection is immensely complicated, so much so that it lies to us and has conditioned us to think that reality is three dimensional. Most of us could swear on the Bible that reality is material. But how can the dimension of a mountain range be materially extant within the scope of the human eye? Can our perception be a deception?

Children have an untutored propensity to run in wonder and embrace the natural world—until they become miseducated by atheism. Little children born in innocence are wonderful theologians! But then they have to go to church and school, which separates them from their capacity to wonder and imagine through an inculcation of fear. It is only when parents, church, and school sever their holographic perspective that disharmony and chaos confuse them.

When, through economic pressures, we disassociate ourselves from our spirituality, we become a house divided from itself. When this happens, we become dualistic on the very grounds through which the cabal of the atheistic new world order wishes to control us. Atheism, through its insistence on objective truth, denies the truth of oneness. Quantum physics informs us that unity is the ground of all being. We are holographic by nature, and there is no separation between spirit and matter. The economy cannot define our eternity. It is precisely because of the dualistic separation which atheism promotes that we become terrified of death. According to atheism, it is only the body that matters; there is no afterlife.

We humans live on the band of our own frequency. Other bands or frequencies can inform us. The relationship between the natural world and humanity is indicative of some superintelligence plan. This world could not be so marvellously arranged without a supermind behind it. The natural world lives on various bands of electricity. This world will experience harmony only when the electromagnetic band of human electricity respects the band which has been assigned to all of creation and not just humans themselves. Viruses of different expressions appear when we do not respect the balance needed for unity within our bodies. Viruses occur and are the secretions of wounded cells attacked by poisons. These viruses are foreign, and a healthy body rejects them as foreign invaders. Atheism is a virus far worse than the coronavirus pandemic, but we pay little attention to it.

The new world order wants to cull the human population by at least five billion, leaving itself as supreme. Because of this plan, it should not be beyond the scope of our imagination to believe that the coronavirus pandemic is more the work of humans than of God.

The vision of Silicon Valley is already realised upon our planet. Robots, smart technology, artificial intelligence, chemical trails, misuse of electromagnetic frequencies, and the internet of things exist among us and are incrementally about to destroy most of humanity. We have become so passive and doped that we are not even aware of our rape. The very nest of our habitat has become overladen with a band of electricity which our human nature can no longer endure or tolerate. Radiation attacks us from every quarter; the manipulation of electromagnetic energy has been twisted for the sake of the atheistic economy and a cashless society. Paper money is deemed a carrier of viruses and must be abolished.

Geoengineering has been happening by a diabolical band of fascists for the past fifty years. We never noticed it simply because we have become anesthetised to our holographic spirituality. The new world order has a different plan in store for us. It has deemed itself superior to the laws of nature and inverted it into a system of capture control and tyranny. When we lose our identity as passionate spiritual beings, we become disconnected.

Death and fear are endemic in all our reactions and perceptions. No matter how we avoid them or cover them up, they always reappear in our considerations and conclusion. The wealthy cabal of atheists have alarmingly infiltrated our imagination and wonder to such a degree that all the dance and poetry of life has been knocked out of us. We preoccupy ourselves with meaningless nothings. We seldom consider the big picture. Through our evolutionary process, we have the choice to stay on the level of natural selection or to rise higher into the sphere of an ultimate omega. Atheistic materialism tethers us to a land where the song of joy and hope is ripped out of it. Atheism is negative and offers the human race only doom and gloom. At the very moment of our death, when we need compassion and encouragement to pass from this world into eternity, it robs us of hope through its stark futility and meaninglessness. Atheism throws acid on our need for purpose in our moment of departure from this world into the next. Just as we have an innate unquenchable longing for a life relieved of our bondage of material anxiety, so too do we have an innate fear of death. Death terrifies us. These two experiences subliminally war with each other every day of our lives. We have been indoctrinated to live on the level of the external, which through Atheistic materialism has gouged or excised the spirit out of us. We have been indoctrinated to avoid pain at all costs, but this very indoctrination is mere escapism. Pain is a very beneficial reality in forging our way through life. It is an alarm bell or a cry for help when our physicality is threatened. Pain is physical; suffering is mental. We have the power within us to transcend our suffering but not our pain. We have the power within us to love or to hate.

We have the power within us to live united or separately. We have the potential within us to submit to all that is flowing and natural, or we can live with the illusion that smart technology will solve all our problems. The intelligence of the human heart does not exist in a robot. The more we seek efficiency and escape through the smart grid, the more we delude ourselves with the false promise of convenience. We can have all the conveniences in our world which are merely external, but if we have not cultivated the internal disposition of appreciation, wonder, and joy within ourselves, then possessions are worthless. It is context that matters and not the content. Seventy per cent of all Americans, the richest country in the world, are mentally suffering and daily try to escape their pain through barbiturates. We have the power within us to choose joy over suffering, but we do not have that same power to erase pain. Pain is necessary and indigenous. Suffering instructs us when used constructively, but we can allow it to not debilitate us. Joy can become our reality when we choose to accept life as fleeting and experiential. Life is fragile, tender, and precious. When we choose suffering over the privilege of living, then we become neurotic. It is precisely because we have been indoctrinated to avoid the pain inscribed and necessary for our welfare that the nature of our human existence becomes inverted.

When spirit and intelligence are removed from consciousness, then only chaos follows. All species in their subhuman existence live exactly in harmony with the electromagnetic energy given to them. They exist in harmony with what is primary in their existence. Humanity, on the other hand, has turned what is primary about us into what is secondary. We have made the body primary and the spirit secondary. We have replaced God with economics. Atheism is our paradigm. Through an incremental and covert system, without even realising it, we are out of tune with all that is natural in our world. We have lost our ability of reverence and respect. We live with the haughtiness of entitlement. Atheism has blocked us from all the invisible reality of consciousness. The atom is almost full of emptiness. We have no definition or understanding of emptiness, yet it is emptiness which best describes us. It is emptiness which surrounds us and upholds us. Emptiness is invisible; we cannot hold it or see it, yet it beholds us. That which is invisible lies beyond the capability of our five senses, yet it is our five senses which disclose to us our living condition. Our senses are limited and cannot tell us we are made for ecstasy. Atheistic materialism has dumbed us down to such a temporal state that we no longer realise we are already eternal. Even though the leaves from our tree may fall and perish, what is essential and central about our tree cannot be disturbed by the terror-stricken plan of arrogant, atheistic humans. The natural world always stays faithful to its own frequency of electricity and sends us millions of messages every day about how we should live according to the light given to us.

Atheism is tyrannical. Truth cannot emanate from dominance. Atheism tries to control nature and turns our subjectivity and interiority into an objective material reality. Atheism causes mental or neurological discourse rather than harmony. Ever since the big bang, our planet has consistently sought, despite its cataclysms, refinement. From the wayward movement of our ancient civilisations, until the enlightenment of the twentieth century, humanity has always given reverence to a higher power. Throughout the centuries, human beings have gained wisdom and truth through the oneness and beauty of nature. Those things now become shrouded in the mystery of the unknown and have shoved the human imagination into the realm of a spiritual reality. Great wisdom has been gained in this evolutionary battle between the known and the unknown. As always, contradictions are refined, and truth comes from contradiction. This has always been the case in the clash of opposites. But when science and religion claim and indoctrinate with certain answers, then humanity becomes victimised. The unknown is an integral part of the human story. Our search is our only answer. Atheism is a choice. But why choose it? It is very negative and ultimately destructive. Both organised religion and atheism are discriminatory. Why choose either of them? It is far better to let God be God and we humans be his children. This way, we place ourselves in the middle between the known and the unknown. This way, our choice is respectful and lacks arrogance. We see ourselves as integrated souls walking on earth with a spirit or consciousness which is eternal. Faith is a choice with the hope of unknowability ingrained in it. The world view which atheism gives is meaningless.

If this experience is so torturous, then what is so terrible about an escape from it despite life's unknowability? Unknowability invites trust, and people who love each other always exercise it in the deep mystery of relationship. Trust links us to one another. Why is it wrong and unenlightened to go on trusting in God despite the fact that our atheistic paradigm teaches the opposite? Why turn life into a dirge rather than a dance? We ourselves decide because of our perspective. As individuals, we can rise us and not allow the killer cult of atheism to deny and denounce all our self-respect and human rights through a power and control system which has never bequeathed to them. There is another way. We can lay down the sword and learn the language of the human heart instead of artificial intelligence and technology.

We have no option but to humbly surrender to unknowability. Humility comes closer to the truth than the arrogant, artificial, human-made configurations. Our so-called progress from the enlightenment into the singularity of our smart technology is an atrocious mistake. It is so calamitous that it will most likely end our presence on this planet. Organised religions which deems themselves to deal with transcendence have been so notoriously silent—and guilty. They are so uninvolved and lacking in moral courage against the sweep and control of atheism that it beggars belief. We are dumbed down and not very well informed. The power and control which mass media has over our minds is so extreme that we have become addicted to false news with which the rich elites indoctrinate us. We are not the product of our own consciousness. We are a desacralised people, but we do not know it. We live according to the tyranny of technology instead of the free choice which theology offers.

The autumn leaves experience an electromagnetic whisper which tells them to dispense with their chlorophyl and prepare for death. How amazing! They do not wail or gnash their teeth in their going; they do not cry or defy. They do not argue with gravity, but one by one they leave their limb of security and, in an arabesque of profound beauty, return to their original ground. Death is ever before us. Atheism considers it an absurdity, but like the autumn leaves, we too can keep a glass of our best wine until last. We too can proclaim a hymn of surrender and trust. Death is but an horizon. We leave the shackles of our troubled bodies behind us and emerge into an eternity of consciousness. The intention of the new world envisions a one-world, global economy and a one-world religion. The elites intend to remove us from nature and move us into mega cities. They intend to prod us like a herd of pigs to a slaughterhouse. Through an electrical invisible attack on the human cell, they produce a virus to weaken and control us into compliance.

The nations of the world will have to borrow huge sums of money which will be loaned through quantitative easing only to push poorer nations into the burden of impossible debt. Through debt, the new world order will own us. Through economy, the spark of spirituality will be eradicated from our perspective. Although the aim of Planned Parenthood, which the Bill Gates Foundation funds, is one of eugenics, the vast majority of the human race refuses to believe in this truth. Planned Parenthood may have changed its language to more subtly mind-control us. The movement of Black Lives Matter is but a ploy in the name of justice and equality, but in fact it perpetuates imperialism through the tactics of divide and conquer. When racism is used as a tactic, both the white race and the coloured race are weakened and robbed of their one true identity as children of God. The consciousness, which quantum physics proposes and advocates for, tells us we are all one. Our battle is not between black and white but between the poor and the privileged. Justice will never occur amongst us until all the races of the earth join in unison against the diabolical pathology of the new world order. A man like Soros, who funds the movement of Black Lives Matter, is interested only in promoting division. The Negro solution remains the same in our contemporary culture amongst the psychopaths of the new world order as it was in the days of black slavery. The real problem is not the division between the races but in the 98 per cent of the world's deprived and the 2 per cent of the elites in the new world order.

The aim of the elitist supremacists is eugenics. The psychopaths of the new world order consider themselves the humans of the social order. They are the survivors and the fittest from the evolutionary struggle. The rest of humanity is but an inferior residue and must be culled. We live in an age when technocracy and transhumanism are all the rage. Humans, instead of God, are now in charge of who should live and who should die! We have become so dumbed down by the elites of the new world order that we now consider the wolves amongst us as our shepherds. Despite the scribbles and empty promises of the new world order, if we as a species are to survive, whether black, brown, yellow, or white, must choose which scripture we will follow. Jesus told us we are a family and that our spirit matters. Our atheistic indoctrination is based on another guiding determinate philosophy. In the words of Margaret Sanger,

> The most merciful thing that the large family does
> to one of its infant members is to kill it
>
> the campaign for birth control
> is not merely of eugenic value
> but is practically identical
> with the final aim of eugenics
>
> All of our problems are the result of overbreeding
> among the working class
>
> We do not want the word to go out
> that we want to exterminate the negro population

Now is the time to awaken to the consciousness within us and fight back. Refuse the perception of racial difference. Refuse to believe in atheism. Refuse to believe that we have no dignity as children of God. Refuse to believe that each one of us is a masterpiece. Refuse to accept that smart technocracy and artificial intelligence can ever define our essence. Refuse to allow 5G technology to destroy us through its radiation.

Two per cent of bandits consider life on our planet to be mere chance. Power and control have invaded their self-concept; they are the agents of our spiritual destruction. The holy name of God has never been concerned or once mentioned in our discussion about the coronavirus. The need for some spiritual assistance in our pandemic crisis seems to have no relevance anymore. God is not mentioned or asked to take care of us during these days of pandemic disturbance. We have become so brainwashed that we no longer have the ability to recognise the connection between the God of consciousness and the real world. We are so dualistic in our media systems, which are owned by a bunch of atheistic psychopaths, that we are scarcely allowed to mention the embrace of a higher, non-local intelligence in our discussions. We are holographic beings, but because of our consciousness, we are spiritual first and human second. We chatter endlessly about the economy and the body but never about our spirituality. The main media does not even have the courage to entertain a program with a spiritual perspective. Instead, it goes on pumping out programmes which desecrate the sacredness of human life. When atheism controls our media, the perception that life is competitive and violent dominates our subconscious. If we as a society could inculcate the spiritual component of our holographic reality, then we would have less suicide in our midst and less need for opiates to give us meaning and hope. Through atheism we become slaves to a diabolical system. The new world order cult of death has denied us the true purpose of electromagnetic information. It has twisted our evolutionary process into something destructive through direct energy weapons. Our smart technology has used the invisible intelligence behind all spiritual reality to their own advantage while denying the invisible reality through which they use it to suit their purposes.

Marshall McLuhan coined the famous phrase "The medium is the message". This message has never been so relevant as it is now in our digitalised age. In this era of smart technology, our machines are co-opting our hearts and minds instead of our hearts and minds co-opting our machines. The elites possess 98 per cent of the world's wealth. Their money buys control and power. Even the very soul of humanity can be bought by money. Corruption is at the very soul of atheism. As one of the Rothschild family declared, "Give me the money, and I care not about the laws of the land." The paradigm of the elites in the new world order is not founded on morality or ethics but most assuredly on profit and money. Cyberspace and the internet of things are owned and operated by a small number of atheistic psychopaths. The hidden state in which they operate exists and is energised by the will to cull the human race. They have covertly and incrementally worked towards the preparation of the soil for a reset of human culture. The elites of the new world order have been so successful and clever in eradicating from the human heart and mind the necessity for a relationship with God, that our dumbed-down minds reject this so-called conspiracy theory as an absurd pack of lies; we are not allowed to entertain this point of view. In Western culture, our problems are never solved holographically—we reject the spiritual dimension. Solutions are always rendered and sought in terms of the external. The priest is called in when the doctor leaves, as if the human person is one-dimensional.

It remains paradoxical that lesser conspiratorial theories than the conspiracy theory about the new world order are allowed some attention in our media. The conspiracy theory surrounding the World Trade Center towers and who shot John F. Kennedy are reluctantly tolerated in our all-consuming media, but to mention the holy name of Yahweh in our discussions is taboo. We pay no attention to the question of meaninglessness with which atheism has indoctrinated us. Gratuitous violence is now the norm of the media as though it were moral and acceptable, especially in the United States. Killing instead of loving is now the message of our media. The message is, "Might is right." Slaughter and mayhem are inverted with the promotion of the message that the good guy always wins, however he can only do it with a gun in his hand. Courage is measured by a machine rather than a person's interior. Gratuitous violence is the greatest sling and arrow ever perpetrated on the human race. We have become so indoctrinated by the message of the media that murder and mayhem are now proposed as the solution to our planet's problems. We have become so dumbed down and indifferent that we have lost our ability to be conscious of our consciousness.

The atheistic, psychopathic elites who control our minds are incapable of compassion and empathy. They look upon us as slaves to enlarge their economy. We are, in the mind of Kissinger, "useless eaters" and, in the mind of Lenin, "blissful idiots". The atheistic new world order has been so successful in its mission to confiscate the wealth and natural gifts of the world that even the right to our singular divinity and sovereignty has been stolen from us. Terrorising our present conditioning is the fact that the plan which these atheistic psychopaths have in store for us has not been fully actualised yet. New vaccines which will poison us are about to be acclaimed as our new saviour, 5G technology will irradiate us, and private property will be misappropriated from us. Like a thirsty doe tempted to drink water at the edge of a lake, we are not aware of the crocodile waiting to leap and devour us. The coronavirus is part of the crocodile's cunning camouflage to destroy us. If we do not awaken to our spirituality, then the water in the lake will become our tsunami. The more we see and understand reality as it is, the closer we come to God. The more we live life in the spectrum of the electromagnetic frequencies with which we are endowed, the closer we come to God. God is the fully illuminated one; we are the shadow from the candle. We are called to cooperate and participate.

The Olympics are based upon the principle of transcendence. Without transcendence, there can be no improvement. An Olympian always attempts to go beyond his or her limits. He or she must be full of commitment, passion, and enthusiasm. The message from the Olympic season is at one with the message of our spirituality. Our attempts may be small but in fact remain our successes. Spirituality defines. We are doomed to attempt to be holy. Our media inculturates us with the opposite messageand teaches us to live on the external level. The message of our enduring eternal and interior spirituality is sacrificed for the sake of accumulating money and profit. This is the greatest of all conspiracies, but we refuse to believe it. The ploys and the hoaxes of the new world order are so heinous that fakery is our new truth and our new Bible. Contemporarily conspiracy theories are considered lies. However, the greatest lie of all is perpetrated by the new world order. It has rewired our minds to think materially rather than spiritually. Our evolutionary process is transcendent by nature; we are part of the eternal consciousness. The new world order tells us a different story.

Never before in the history of our planet have psychotic humans enacted laws to control and survey us. Transhumanism and smart technocracy are already involved in the destruction of the human family. Social credit will be meted out to us according to the law laid down by the elite rather than our own conscience.

The coronavirus is a covert and incremental step hammered out at Davos to further terrorise us. The threat is much more about surveillance and control than it is disease and viruses. Those who oppose the tactics and lies of the elite—namely, the conspiratorial remnant—are considered misfits, troublemakers, and demented. As I will explain later in this book, reality is only actualised by a clash of opposites. This is called the paradox of polarity. A typed book with black ink is best seen when it is printed on a white background. Contraries are complementary. Atheism compels us to question the reality of God. As Wordsworth said, "There is more faith in doubt than in all the creeds of man." Nothing is definite in this world. It is our perception which makes the affairs of life reasonable and acceptable. If this be so, then why are conspiracy theories never allowed to challenge the atheistic status quo?

If corruption decadence, inequality, and injustice, which are the expressions of our interior human disposition, can be so easily accepted and tolerated, then why is the interior disposition of our spirituality dismissed as nefarious and a hindrance to the human process? Who is the madman when pathological elites pay scientific specialists to announce to the world a message of deceit in compliance with their own biased conclusions? Why should we enact new laws which further ensnare us and destroy the human right to free speech and justice? Some scientists will sell their souls when offered an exorbitant amount of money for the endorsement of the new world order. The price of consent is compensation. This is the method of arrogant men who live and die in fakery. Take for instance Monsanto and the tobacco industry. If conspiratorial theories are so false, then why are they never even mentioned, discussed, or dismissed on our media channels? Could it be that the new world order does not want us to awaken to the potentiality of our consciousness? Spirituality is dangerous! Atheism thrives on ignorance and misinformation as much as it does on money and profit.

It is we the people who already have within us that one great antigen to fight corruption and disease. If we were to awaken and recover our consciousness, then a new springtime of green grass and leaves would blossom on our original ground. God would reincarnate us. We have been indoctrinated and dumbed down to not recognise our true possibilities. We desperately search for antiviral drug to erase COVID-19. If we awaken, we will find this recreated earth within us; it is called spirituality.

A band of vipers has taken cyber control over the cosmos, and with their direct energy weapons, they can selectively and invisibly target any nation or ethnic group upon the planet. Technology has become so sophisticated that simulation is now possible. Lip movement can be synchronised with words a politician or president never said. Fake news has become triumphant in new ways. Drones are now used for spying purposes. Direct energy weapons are invisible, microwaved, and wireless.

The elites of the new world order offer humanity an utopia of heaven on earth through the internet of things and smart technology, only to deliver a hell on earth through their ensnarement. The new world order has inscribed its intention on the Georgia Guidestones; all that is needed is our acquiescence.

A cabal of wealthy, atheistic psychopaths control all of cyberspace. Its members represent 2 per cent of the human population. Like a Trojan Horse, they remain as a statue to our sight, but inside, like a brood of vipers, they are ready to inflict Armageddon on the human race. We inhabitants of a global earth are held in ransom by this 2 per cent of diabolical men. Because they own 98 per cent of the world's wealth, they presume they alone are the survivors of the fittest. The rest of humanity is but the offal of the evolutionary process. We are the ones who did not make it. We are the vanquished ones in the war of survival of the fittest. We are the lame and the crippled. We are the ones who did not have the necessary mental capacity to reach the top echelon of society. We are the losers in the evolutionary war for survival. For too long, we have been allowed to live indiscriminately and pollute the environment like copulating rabbits. We are a virus upon the face of the earth. We are useless eaters pressuring the earth into an unsustainable future.

Because this 2 per cent of a self-canonised bunch of atheistic psychopaths could not possibly kill off the 98 per cent of the rest of humanity through a cataclysmic event, they have chosen instead to eliminate most of us in a covert and incremental way. They have cleverly used weather control and the employment of a virus to terrify us into submission. Little do we realise there are strands of further control in the web of their vision. Unless we detect this elephant in our living rooms, further strangulations and control over our bodies await us. This may happen in an accelerated way because of the triumph and success with which the coronavirus has managed to terrify us. This atheistic death cult is the elephant in our living space which is silently and stealthily about to destroy us. A cashless society and an overload of radiated electricity through smart technology are covert means to take total control over our bodies.

This same cult of death employs the electromagnetic invisible field to kill us, and it concomitantly dismisses all reality which is not rational and objective. Surely invisibility has as much potency within it to direct humanity to a higher source of intelligence than atheism warrants. Even though atheism uses the invisibility of electromagnetic waves to terrify us through weather control and viruses, why cannot the human race protest that the invisibility of the very opposite can save us?

The problem confronting us is that the paradigm of atheism which now rules our perception has cleverly infiltrated into the holographic resolution of human existence. It has evicted the spirituality of our perception out of existence. Atheism has destroyed our balance between immanence and transcendence. It has made the our bodies into a scheme of having and doing. We have become so dumbed down about the eternity of our consciousness that we are incapable of connecting our present crises with the intervention of our spiritual potency.

The intention of this atheistic death cult is to squeeze every fibre of spirituality out of us. It has insidiously infiltrated not only the human family but also the Vatican. Paedophilia and pornography are part of their plan to destroy the values of Western civilisation. Through transhumanism, fascist atheistic man can now create in its battery of hatcheries new humans with no specific gender attached to them. Through a transmorphic manipulation, we are already experiencing through specific drugs a world infused with transgenderism. Ours will be a planet with no specific gender upon it. We acquiesce through our silence. We accept under the perception of progress. Without a baa of protest, we follow a shepherd who is in reality a butcher. The world information forum which gathers at Davos is a sham. It is nothing more than a meeting where the wealthy of the earth gather to congratulate each other for their exploitation of the earth and the enslavement of the rest of us. Theirs is a world of technocracy instead of theology.

Spirituality is the only reality which releases us from the anxiety and bondage of the human body. Pandemic viruses terrify us into a state of isolation and desolation. Pandemic viruses separate us. Pandemic viruses are caused by a death cult; they are the result of an atheistic vision for the planet. Pandemic viruses violate the very fabric of life which quantum physics proclaims to be unitive. The death cult of the new world order destroys the balance between our bodies and our spirits. Spirituality is necessary for our holographic perspective. Our crisis is spiritual. Yet disastrously, all the commentators, psychologists, medical professionals, and journalists have never once mentioned the sacred name of God in all their discussions about our coronavirus disaster. All our considerations in the media centre on economic problems, however unless the immateriality of our existence is considered, there are no conclusions or lasting resolutions if the divine within us is included and brought to the table. We all have a fear of death and the unknown. Atheism uses this fear to terrify us. The balance which our innate spirituality gives us transcends our postage-stamp understanding of reality and gives us answers more redolent with meaning and promise than the politics of man. In the midst of our sorrows, the indiscriminate message of our spirituality tells us that we are eternal consciousness. Our inner being proclaims we are of supreme importance. Atheism essentially proclaims we are worthless.

If we are not to perish, it is time to live by a spiritual paradigm. By no means does this mean we should re-establish the power and control of organised religion, which is as dualistic as atheism. Unity instead of separation is the direction our emergent church must realise. Despite our cultural and tribal differences, we are all children of the one God. So long as the love and compassion of this same God unites us, then surely there cannot be fundamental differences between us. God is our common denominator, and without divinity's presence in all our considerations, peace and harmony cannot be realised on our planet.

In a world gone mad from the indoctrination of atheism, the preceding ramblings may only be considered a conspiracy theory. However, in this age of false news, may we not at least question the falseness of perception? Perhaps the greatest conspiracy of all is that atheism is the paradigm best suited for intelligent and informed humanity. How can truth be found except by the honest and refining questions of an opposing point of view? There is an arsis and thesis in all reality. Contraries are complementary. Does faith in a great ineffable, non-local intelligence not have as much validity as the opposing view of atheism? The paradox of polarity is the source of all credibility.

The conspiracy of faith and spirituality today could possibly be tomorrow's truth and the humility of surrender to the incomprehensible. God may as yet not be finished with his creation. Maybe the clay in the potter's hand will become a jug or a cup full of grace compassion and forgiveness. Why are whistle-blowers always tortured? Why does the mere word *conspiracy* always have a pejorative notion attached to it? Could it possibly be that those who, through their indoctrination, have convinced others that their own corruption and thievery is the truth? Could it be that atheism is the most pejorative conspiracy theory of all? Could the conspirator of today be tomorrow's whistle-blower? As individual spiritual beings, we can do little to oppose the consuming control of atheism, but we can be messengers who can change the world as Christ did. In the words of Oscar Wilde, "The pen is mightier than the sword." In our contemporary atheistic culture, truth is treated as discriminatory and prejudiced. Censorship and suppression has become the new art form of journalism. Only those who own the media excuse themselves from censorship. A hidden cabal of atheistic indoctrinators determine and shape our perceptions. As Henry Kissinger said, "It is the perception and not the truth which matters." As a consequence, our modern world is more addicted to suppression than it is to the expression of the truth. Suppression and censorship are much more about power and control of free speech. In the name of hate speech, it is cosmically brutal in suppressing questions and investigations which are part and parcel of legitimate enquiry. Censorship and suppression reflect more on the giver than the receiver. Those who postulate it are in fact the very people who most fear it. They protect themselves with falsity rather than truth. Those who rage on about conspiracy theories are often themselves the greater threat to human society. They keep us all in total confusion and anxiety. They have inverted all our perceptions for the sake of profit and money. They themselves are the true moguls of dishonesty. They have lulled us all into a false economy. A humanity separated from its spirituality is the playground for the elite. It becomes easier to profit from humanity's slavery when we exchange our spirituality for the pittance of a false economy. Banks have no spires which pierce the heavens.

For the first time in our history, we have witnessed the consequence and horrific destruction which the splitting of the atom has caused us. From the moment of its construction, we have used up a massive amount of human energy to control it. Our total concern lies within the secondary realm of our egoic and material world. Having bitten of the forbidden apple, we do not know how to handle its consequences, so we have managed to keep its overflow in barrels of cold storage. The primary membrane of concern for the nucleus of the atom has not yet been considered by the atheistic men of science, who have dwelt too much on the effect rather than the nucleus which caused it. We know much about radiation but little about the sun, which causes it. We limit our attention to the reality of our anthropology. We dabble with effects instead of causes. All that exists materially has its counterpart in spirituality. Life is holographic. This is the universal truth of nature, and whether we like it or not, there is no escape from it. What we brush out through the front door comes rushing in through the back door. Divinity, like water, always seeks out its own level. Though atheism erects sandbags to block its flow, God's ascendent reality will always surround and surmount it. Whenever and wherever the divine becomes absent or minimised in our world, a state terrorised by fear soon arises. The fear of nuclear power which now controls us has become our reality because of the stupidity of human hubris. Atheistic men of science have removed God from nucleus of our meaning and purpose. The fear of God is constructive and balanced. The fear which man causes through his disturbance of the nucleus is lethal and dangerous. If the Christian church is ever to become more concerned in an interpenetrative way, then it must vociferously preach the fear of God's justifiable anger and wrath against our ill will rather than preoccupy its attention with incomprehensible dogmas such as the Virgin Mary's immaculate conception.

There have been moments of singularity in the history of homo sapiens, such as the invention of the wheel and the printing press. These revolutionary occurrences have benefited the progress of our evolutionary story to a magnificent degree. Very lately, however, in the four-million-year history of our species, we have turned our sight away from transcendence and imagined ourselves as the cause of our own creation. For this very reason, our singular inheritance is the bond we bear to our materiality. Accordingly, atheistic science proclaims that human life is non-emergent and ends with a senseless stopgap measure. There is no explanation other than the fact that we exist without rhyme or reason. Because life is unreasonable, in our stupor we think we have the right to weaponise the atom's nucleus. With this choice, we have reached the zenith of man's corruptible ability to master nature. If the truth of such a decision be known, what we have, be it for egotistical or national reasons, will ultimately destroys all our positive geoengineering projects.

It has taken thousands of years for Homo sapiens to undergo moments of singularity which advance and assist our human condition, but now atheistic science has offered the human race two powerful singularity moments in the space of a few years. Atheistic science appears to be much more efficient and consistent in the law of supply and demand within the sphere of the material. In the mere span of a minute, nuclear weapons can eliminate and destroy all the struggles of the empty microbial atom as it proceeds on its evolutionary journey toward natural selection. Science has already proven this at Hiroshima. However, no matter its power of destruction on the atomic physical level, it still cannot destroy the microbiology of spirituality as it flows and is absorbed by consciousness. What is divine, though it exists in the atom, still vibrates without it. A transformation occurs. The old world gives way and withers for the sake of a fuller divine experience. As it is on earth, so spirit abides in heaven. Divinity always exists and cannot be limited.

Terrifying as the singularity of atomic weaponry is, within the space of a few years, another singularity moment of surprise and deadly consequence has already appeared on our horizon. Like the weather control problem, one storm after another now seems to arise out of nowhere. Our latest singularity moment was born and promoted by Silicon Valley. Its name is artificial intelligence, or AI for short. As we will discover later in this book, atheistic materialism ends our epic evolutionary story with its chapter in the middle on natural selection. When the prospect of a higher reality is connected to our physicality, then money and profit become secondary. When economy is primary, the men who own 98 per cent of the world's wealth will not surrender or let go of their privileged position. That is why the holy name of God or the prospect of a divine presence at work in this world is not tolerated on our communication channels. As long as corrupt men control the propaganda and infect our minds with the virus of atheism, this world will never be the holographic reality God intended it to be.

Desecrated and dumbed down as we are, we do not realise that the singularity of AI and smart technology have been engineered not to free us but to control and have power over us. Because of the internet of things, which falsely offers us a paradise of freedom from our daily chores and routine, we become instead subjects to an unsympathetic overlord without a consideration for our emotions. Digitalisation demolishes and dismisses divinity. No matter our experimentation with microbiology, there is no sympathy or compassion within it.

Not only will the singularity of AI destroy our individuality, but socially atheistic science, just as it weaponised the nucleus of the atom, will also weaponise the information of electromagnetic energy for national and egoic reasons rather than for the universal geoengineering purpose of universal love.

We do not seem to recognise that the lockdown caused by the coronavirus is the first real unfolding of a singular technological plan by the atheistic kill cult to genocide us. Unless we break out from the isolation and separation which the coronavirus has caused, we will become even more victimised by the rich, psychopathic elite who plan to eliminate five billion of the planet's people. We think that after the coronavirus has gone, we will return to normal. On the contrary, the full blast of a weakened economy awaits us. Our immune system has been already weakened by the coronavirus, but a more virulent attack on our cells is planned through 5G technology. We are the receivers of the radiation poured down on us from satellites with which Elon Musk has saturated the skies above us. 5G technology is designed to kill us. It is a distortion of the electromagnetic information which nature intends for us. 5G is the most potent destructive force imposed on humans since the atomic bomb. Already the killer cult has already created a bubble of radiation above us, and we, the poor of the earth, are its target. 5G technology is an energy lasered together by evil men for unnatural, diabolic reasons. When our cells are targeted with 5G radiation, they will not be capable of creating an immunity capable of fighting off its invasion. The human body does not have the capability to adjust to such a viral infection. Unless we cease to be acquiescent, cancer will grow ever more rampant in our midst as a consequence.

> For evil to triumph, all that is necessary
> Is for good men to do nothing.
> —Edmund Burke

The elite, killer cult who represent just 2 per cent of the world's population have inverted God's Lordship over the universe. It is we who are allowing these psychopaths to accomplish terrifying agenda through our passivity.

When AI and electromagnetic energy are used competitively as war weapons, then they become one of the most singular tools for domination, suppression, and oppression.

Death terrifies us. Atheistic men build their edifice around this fact. They are experts in dispelling it from our observation, yet they use it. To counteract the awful message of atheism's theodicy, we can perceive reality differently. Indeed, the urging of the human mind for a happy ending to our story, is, despite Freud's musings far more beneficial to the allotment of our humanity than the indoctrination of atheism. Death is the great adieu. Death is saying goodbye to the body and hello to God. Our inconsolable longing through its very residual presence in our brains is itself a proof that death is not an ending in itself. Why would nature leave such a residue of uncertainty within the human psyche without a benign resolution? To do so would make our story an unfinished symphony. Death is the call of the strings in our concerto's call of the violin. Some incomprehensible reality leaves the human body at the moment of death. This emptying out is so elusive that no chemical solution can be reasonably found to retain or recapture it. Neither does the discipline of rational mathematical science seem to be capable of explaining it. The fact is this one great emptying of life remains unsolved and insolvable without hope in our belief system.

Atheism postulates itself as the most sophisticated scholar on the subject of death, but in fact it is a diseased and deceptive interloper. The solution to the problem lies with our understanding of oneness and isness. Even atheism cannot rationally give the necessary proof or the absence of this isness. Atheistic rational science demands of the other objective proof, but concomitantly it cannot objectively prove the veracity in its own process of truthfulness. Without music, there can be no sound—but without sound, there can be no music. Atheism denies the inner music of the spheres because it does not have the will or tolerance to listen to it. If, for the sake of its own hubristic or perhaps agnostic stance, atheism were to shut its mouth completely regarding its infantile answer of chance and randomness, it would serve its own cause more truthfully and artfully. Because the theodicy of atheism centres on the reality of materiality, it has no right to impose its own conclusions on a discipline which lies outside its competence. It is precisely because atheism has run like a virus through the reality of humanity's spirituality that the human condition has become so toxic.

Any regiment or theodicy which neglects humanity's holography infects and causes a dystopia AI because it is artificial and is not really relevant to the way God has eternally created us. When we dismiss God's involvement in the arena of human politics, then we end up with a self-creating universe.

We are daily given messages and sights in the midst of the ordinary occurrences of our daily lives only we fail to make a connection to a higher and more pregnant reality. We are presently confronted by the presence of a tiny invisible reality called the coronavirus. We are compelled to use a microscope to uncover its mystery. Yet this tool only allows us see its surface reality whereas in fact this tiny particle composed of emptiness and invisibility has the potency to stop the commercial interflow and interface between all the nations of the earth. Bridges depend on the support of pebbles. Birth cannot arise out of competition. Material wellbeing cannot be accomplished fruitfully without the balance of and cooperation of the human spirit. There is a presence more awesome and powerful in the spirit of man than he can ever dream of. What is essential is invisible.

Death

Through death, we, the loved ones who follow after those who have begotten us through our hope and faith, turn the past into the present as though the mortal is immortal. This capacity of the human mind to turn illusion into reality is perhaps in itself a true expression of God's continuous presence in our death moments. Often in our most painful experiences, when God seems absent, we begin to hear a different voice than the one which our degrading atheistic matrix megaphones to us. Often through the din and the noise of our atheistic paradigm, God uses our little tongues to speak an immortal message. How often do we say, "I can't believe he's dead", "Where do you think you're going?" "Who do you think you are?" "I feel her presence everywhere?" and "She's in every room of the house"? such primal remarks may only be superstitious, yet at the same time they may well be the inward voice of divinity speaking to us about the eternity and immateriality of consciousness. Our moments of desolation can become an experience of consolation, if we will it. It is only when we fail in our attempts to comply with the false indoctrination and distractions of materialistic atheists that the God of absence will become present. Atheists, such as Richard Dawkins in his book *The God Delusion*, insist that unless a rational evidence for the existence of God can be given, we must conclude that God does not exist. However, theism can use the same argument against atheism by demanding a rational proof for the non-existence of a higher intelligence. Indeed, it would seem that the existence of God is more likely to be true because of all the clues which we find in the routine of our daily lives. There are millions of applications beyond reason that suggest the existence of transcendence which exists in the everyday harmony of the universe. There is too much wonder in our world to conclude with certainty that God does not exist.

Take for instance the machinery involved in our own human bodies. We ourselves are the greatest proof on earth that some non-local intelligence created us. It is impossible to comprehend that we came into this world out of mere chance and randomness. No matter the claim of atheism, it makes much more sense to say there is something rather than nothing. Otherwise, how can we explain why or how life on our planet was created? We may not be able to explain God, but that does not give us permission to reject him. Atheism deflects not only contemplation on the machinery of our bodies but also the spiritual complementation within them.

The Human Cell

The human cell is mind-boggling. All the difference between living and non-living happens in a circumference not much bigger than a pinpoint. The most dramatic and awe-inspiring force in this world is not the eruption of volcanoes, the rush of the tsunami, or the terrifying power of the tornado, but the splitting of the cell into two.

A single cell, when observed microscopically, is a metropolis as complex as any teeming city. Each cell has its own moat of protein called an enzyme. This membrane regulates with gates whatever enters or leaves the cell. The enzyme allows the essential nutrients to enter the cell. What the cell accomplishes in seconds would take weeks for a well-equipped chemical factory to synthetically produce.

Each cell has its own transportation system, library of information, and police force. Each cell has its own energy created by a powerhouse called mitochondria. Each cell has its own factories (called ribosomes) and recycling plants (called lysosomes). In effect, each cell is a city made up of a hundred thousand atoms. The human body is composed of red and white cells. The red corpuscles oxygenate, and the white cells immunise the system from invading antigens. They are made in the marrow of the bone and rush to defeat a foreign intruder.

How can we possibly demand objective evidence for the existence of God when subjectively, so much mystery, wonder, and awe confront us?

> The cell gives us a view of unparalleled complexity- a world of supreme technology …
> we see that nearly every feature of our own advanced machines
> has its analogue in the cell …
> what we witness is an object resembling an immense automated factory—
> A factory larger than a city
> and carrying out as many unique functions
> as all the manufacturing activities of man on earth.
> —Michael Deuton

Mystery is packed mystically and minuscule. All the full-blown music from the orchestras of the planet depends on a scale of seven notes. The human brain, through synapses, makes thirteen trillion connections every day, which immeasurably outstrips all the calls humans make on their iPhones every day. Our brains make a thousand connections every second, but we miss the vast majority of them. Nanotechnology can never outsmart the human brain with its efficiency. Atheistic men think they can outperform the mind of God in the puniness of their inflated artificial intelligence.

Human-Made Factories

A human-made chemical factory covering ten thousand acres with the most sophisticated technology has not yet managed to produce the non-addictive drugs created in the three-pound weight of the human brain. The human brain produces narcotics twice as potent as any we can buy in a chemist shop. Narcotics such as serotonin are non-additive and given to us freely.

The Human Heart

The human heart, weighing less than one pound, pumps about six tons of blood over more than sixty thousand miles of the circulatory system every day. The heart moves seventy-five million gallons of blood with its life-sustaining oxygen and nutrients.

Without the imprint of this intelligence, nothing exists.

> Some people see things and ask why?
> But I dream dreams that never were and ask
> why not?
>
> Must a Christ die in every generation
> for those who have no imagination!
> —George Bernard Shaw

As we will see later in our chapter on Irish spirituality there is only a thin line between an earthly and heavenly reality. Immanence and transcendence are joined together. There is no separation between the here and the hereafter; the eternal swallows up the temporal. Our anthropocentric perceptions are an illusion. The human mind manufactures them because we cannot imagine a time or a space beyond our present experience. We need intuition and imagination to catapult us into such an alien reality. It is our artistic capability, which is far more enlarging than our rationality, that ushers us into the realm of divine possibility. Analytical rationality is cold, flat, and land-laden, whereas the power of our spirituality analysis enables us to fly into the starry expanse of the universe.

Apart from the human imagination and intuition's disposition to indicate the possibility of God's existence to us, the many fantastic occurrences within nature, which surround us daily, may not give us rational proof. But by their complex wonder and appearance, they give us a clue. We will deal with some of ordinary life's wonders as reasonable indicators for God's existence in later chapters.

Apart from the mystery of the ordinary, the unreasonable demand of atheism is its own nemesis. In and of its very existence, because of the paradox of polarity, atheism serves a purpose in the sense that it cleanses and challenges the certainty of organised religion. It cries out against the hypocrisy of a church consumed with its own interests and a sense of arrogant supremacy.

We humans are limited by the time and space of our bodies. Our now is challenged by our how. We think anthropocentrically simply because our present experience is all we know, and we measure reality by our perception of it. This is the precise mindset of atheism. Through its insistence on the experience of perception as the only valid explanation for human reality, it totally ignores all those experiences which make human life worth living. It reduces life to material things with no sense of spirit within them. Atheism makes the transcendentals of the one, the true, and the beautiful subjugated to its own puny dimension of economy. Atheism, through its insistence on objective, rational proof for the existence of a transcendent reality, makes a mockery out of our unquenchable longing for something greater. Atheism is destructive of the human imagination. It denies the possibility of divinity sensed through intuition. While it offers us quick solutions for our comfort and convenience, it sows and cultivates a dystopian reality which future generations will have to endure. When a house is built on sand, one day its construction will end only in desolation and destruction. Foundations built on shaky grounds always fall and fail because of their false premises. Without intuition and imagination, there can be no music or poetry in life. Creativity is seeded not by chance but by the dance.

Deception

Certainty has not proven itself to be a good word in the annals of human history. Atheism spells trouble for the human story because of its fundamental certainty. We humans have no moral compass to guide us because the horsemen of atheism stand ready to shoot us if we attempt to escape their entrapment. They already have the advantage from their superior position of power on the backs of their white horses, so we are considered little more than sheep ready to be slaughtered. We have been meticulously, decisively, covertly, and incrementally led to our position of helplessness. We no longer have a good shepherd to guide us. We have forfeited the right to consciousness which evolution has given us. Deceptive, psychotic, atheistic men, for the sake of their own economy, have taken our divine birth right away from us. To these supremacists, we are simply animals. This is psychological fascism. Atheism is as certain of its own doctrine as is Christian fundamentalism. Both systems are closed, uncompromising, and unquestioning. We are too exclusive, discriminatory, racist, uninspired, linear, literal, and unredemptive in the interpretation of our own Bible of life. Both atheism and Christian fundamentalism decentralise the ache of the human heart for purpose and meaning. Neither system respects the idea that revelation is ongoing. One generation provides us with a new door into another room of exploration. God is not finished with us yet. So long as we dismiss conclusion and certainty, new possibilities provide us with information and answers.

Both Christian fundamentalism and atheism are anti-informational. They interfere with the spiritual reality of electromagnetic frequencies. Christian fundamentalism puts an end to the flow of energy's capacity to bring us new information, whereas atheism denies the invisible spiritual dimension to its reality. Worse still, the pomposity, arrogance, and petty minds of atheistic scientists have dared to control and direct the incommunicable and inconceivable reality of energy in such a way that it is becoming more destructive rather than constructive. According to our scientific understanding, electromagnetic energy gives us all our information. How we use it determines our future. It is invisible and spiritual by its very nature, but it impacts our bodily reality in the most intimate and radical way. By its very nature, electromagnetic frequencies have a most intimate and radical connection with our bodily functions. For this reason alone, it is imperative that the discipline of science must work in conjunction with its spiritual counterpart to offer humanity its holographic complementation. Our greatest tragedy is that in our evolutionary progress into full integration, atheistic science has refused to join body and spirit. It makes the attempt to make this connection unnatural and stupid. Atheistic materialists know very well that as the quotient of spirituality increases, so too will the decadence of our matrix decrease. A drugged society is a society which no longer knows its need for God. It is a society in search of its own divinity;

atheism has robbed it of this conviction. Psychiatry and world governments in general, so long as they refuse to recognise the holographic nature of humanity, will continue to administer miles of bandages to pinpricks of damage and only a little Band-Aid to our gushing arteries. We have arrived at such an impasse in modern society that the ownership of our conscious divinity is never recognised or mentioned. This is psychological fascism. This pressure to conform to an atheistic paradigm is strengthened by parents who want us to conform rather become human beings who think outside the box. By the age of four, we are already conformists, although we may not be verbally capable of expressing our self-concept. It is far easier to be an American, a German, an Italian, or an Irishman than it is to be a Christian.

Fundamental Option

Good or evil will cohabit our spirit according to the perception of our own consciousness. Truth no longer matters when perception overrules and poisons us. That is why atheism has had such an imprint on our daily existence. For too long, we have allowed what is inferior to contaminate the higher self. We fail to recognise that what we perceive is mostly illusionary and external instead of interior and subliminal. Herein lies the perennial clash of opposites. Our greatest challenge lies in the fundamental option. Is life meaningful, or is it absurd? Atheism mocks meaning and attends only to the demands of immanence. It dismisses transcendence as wishful, irrational thinking. It promotes having and consuming as the only rational reason for living. It indoctrinates us to eat, drink, and be merry, for tomorrow we die. Cooperation becomes corporation and compassion becomes competition in the atheist's dictionary. The only ascension worth striving for is the assumption and resurrection of a corrupt economy. Atheism conquers through division. It prizes the affairs of the body to the detriment of the human spirit. It promises an instant Christmas without the mindful preparation of advent. Atheism inverts reality. Through indoctrination and mind control, it has commodified the human person into a greedy, devouring monster and objects of attraction to address their insatiable needs.

Atheism claims life has no meaning and has evolved by chance. Those who have faith, love, and hope think differently. The only positive contribution which atheism affords to society is what we might call the paradox of polarity. Every reality in this world has the potentiality of its opposite within it. A white paper communicates nothing unless blackness or darkness is inscribed with an imprint upon it. Light and dark must intermingle before the miracle of enlightenment happens. Contraries are complementary and necessary. Though religion preaches mostly the wrong rendition of God's presence amongst us, it postulates some faith and hope for our future. For this reason alone, organised religion, despite its dualism, offers to the human race a nuanced redemption. Even to the receptor of a minimalist intelligence, it is far better to process life with faith and hope than to endure it without them. On a rational level, it seems evident from a purely psychological level that faith, hope, and love give a powerful resonance and assistance to the human experience. When we value these three transcendentals, life becomes more bearable and endurable. When we have a why, we have a purpose. People who suffer from serious depression constantly tell us that mind pain is unalterably more injurious and vicious than physical suffering. Freud, considered one of the greatest gurus in our contemporary atheistic culture, claimed that religion is but an opiate. It comes from the unconscious need of a child's wish for security.

Neither atheism nor religion give us a satisfactory answer to the question of life's purpose and meaning. As long as men dwell on the level of the seeming alone, as long as they simulate rather than stimulate the human mind, human nature remains bereft of answers which address our mystery. Like an iceberg, there is a lot more to our circumference than that which appears on top of the water. There is a paradox at work in the uncovering of our true identity. What this world needs more than anything else is the courage and effort we must make to become counterculture. The iceberg must be turned upside down so that what is deepest about us will come to the surface. Our transcendentals must be ploughed into our soil so that what is beyond, beneath, above, and around us may find the space to live within us. When this becomes our new normal instead of the technology of atheism, then the earth will be filled with a new revelation and a new hospitality.

I saw a stranger yestereen;
I put food in the eating place
Drink in the drinking place
music in the listening place
and in the blessed name of God.
He blessed myself and my house
my cattle and my dear ones.
And the lark said in her song
"often often, often" goes the Christ
in the stranger's guise
"often, often. Often"
goes the Christ in the stranger's guise
—Old Irish rune of hospitality

It is only through our own balance that an at-one-ment with our one, true, and beautiful reality is possible. We are made in the image of God. This is a gratitudinous gift. Nature itself demands gratefulness, reverence, appreciation, and adoration. If we do not conform to the command of worship, then only isolation and annihilation awaits us.

Jesus said, "By your fruits you shall know them." It seems perfectly clear that our present atheistic matrix is offering us a modified fruit which is poisoning us. Atheism has duped us into eating and swallowing the forbidden fruit in the Garden of Eden. We have failed to realise there is more to life than meets the eye. We judge by externals. Every object which looks red and rosy appeals to our senses, and we want to immediately add it to our larder. We must have it. It looks shiny and perfectly proportioned. In our contemporary Western culture, we have a long, shady history in our record of grasping and exploitation. Like trained zealots, we have been conditioned to bark and grasp the fish which our controlling masters have thrown at us. We accept without question the power with which our atheistic and religious leaders indoctrinate us. If there is one feature which distinguishes us from the subhuman animal kingdom, it must surely be our intelligence. Of all animals on this planet, we humans are the first to realise our consciousness. Even Darwinian evolution admits this. Atheism insists that survival of the fittest and natural selection explain the fullness of the human story. Our history is purely on the horizontal and material level. The ants on our tree have taken away our leaves. Our only purpose is to be gnashed into fodder.

Such a rendition of the human story is surely frightening and nightmarish. But then, when we think more clearly, the turning of pages in the atheistic evolutionary story is cleverly and opportunistically adapted to fit the pernicious intention of the atheistic power structure which governs us. When atheism becomes superpowerful through the exploitation of the environment and the superabundance of money, then economy becomes the content of life. Ordinary civilians, when robbed of their spiritual identity, become slaves to a system which ignores the sacredness and dignity of the human person. By controlling the economy, atheism squeezes all of the divinity out of humanity. The human race has become so alienated from our holographic perspective that we might as well have gone backwards to a lower step on the evolutionary ladder. This is where the atheistic elite who own 98 per cent of the world's wealth wish us to remain. Neither the Church nor the state wish us to become more integrated and intelligent in concern for our own evolutionary story. Through a total emphasis on the economy, our present matrix exercises more abusive and corrupt excesses in human savagery. With our disassociation from our interior divinity, our culture becomes ever more diabolical. Some social critics and mystics have warned us that we have already lost our balance and veered too far towards the sensate. Social critics tell us we have reached the point of no return. It all depends on the vindication of God from now on. Most certainly it would seem if we are to move from the sensate into the ideational, then we must learn to deal a death blow to the paradigm of atheism.

Manifestations of the Divine

> Full many a flower
> is made to bloom unseen
> and waste its sweetness on the desert air
> —William Wordsworth

> Shall I take the rainbow out of the sky
> and the moon from the well in the lane
> and break them in pieces to coax your eye
> to slumber
> a while again!
> —Francis Ledwidge

> It is only the children who know what
> they are looking for
> —Antoine de Saint-Exupéry

Our terrible tragedy is that we understand so little about ordinary life. Because of indoctrination, we fail to make the connection between the here and the hereafter. We have become so uneducated and dumbed down spiritually that the same one consciousness unites under and over, inner and outer. The same one reality runs on like a river in and through its higher resolution. The water of the river goes on singing the same song in the sea of its consummation. Nothing is separate. There are many streams alive in the one sea, but there is only one sea, which provides refuge and containment for all the little streams of the world.

There are millions of little rivers and streams running through the tweed fabric of our planet, but we fail to see the different flecks in the one shawl. We are meant by nature to contemplate, to behold the birds of the air and the lilies of the field, but we have been so maligned and distracted psychologically that we are not only removed from the photosynthesis of nature but also the insurmountable wisdom and wonder of our own bodies. We automatically breathe in oxygen without even a moment of reverence and thanksgiving. The only time we seem to fully appreciate ordinary life is at that moment when we are on the edge of losing it. We reserve our most profound capacity for believing when sensational events of spiritual consequence seem to be actualised. At the same time, we take for granted and ignore all the unsensational miracles of the ordinary in our everyday lives. To be truly spiritual is to realise that the birth of our own child is much more impressive than a thousand miracles of changing water into wine or a hundred miracles of Mary's apparitions to unsuspecting peasant children.

Spirituality arises out of an ache, when we begin to suspect the randomness with which atheism addresses the human predicament. Randomness destroys the possibility of creativity. Randomness postulates only death. There is no possibility for good within it, yet our culture devotes most of its energy towards the endurance of its bankruptcy. By our very nature, we are attracted to beauty. As Dostoyevsky said, "Beauty shall save the world." Our endless restlessness, at its very core, is in itself a proof of God's existence. If there is no God, then why do we yearn? There resides within us an aching need for the Infinite. Our physical attraction to objects of external beauty has its template in our interior. The more we reconcile our sense of external beauty with a sense of interiority, the more our experience of human love will become a part of an ecstatic divine love. The randomness and chance which atheism proposes retards and destroys our mortal creativity, whereas beauty intensifies our enthusiasm with passion and meaning. Atheism has yet to produce a poem or a dance. It offers nothing but gloom to humanity. The human person becomes truly beautiful in terms of his or her spiritual reality. There is no disclosure value in atheism. It is a dark and ugly force which destroys the theopoetic evidence of a supreme intelligence holding in balance our incredible planet and universe. The preoccupation which we render to our egotistical needs muffles the sound of our need for transcendence. For this reason, we remain restless and unintegrated. We become a house divided, never at ease with the fact that we are doomed to be spiritual. but we must bow bend our heads in wonder if we are to live integral lives.

We humans do not know, and perhaps never will know, how the mustard seed propelled itself into infinity. However, we cannot declare that there is no imaginative creative being beyond this mystery. If there is no God, then why or how are we here? The more science uncovers the reality of our earth, the more it confirms the workings of a superior creative designer. Atheism rejects this argument and posits the absurd argument of randomness instead. The fine-tuning involved in the creation of the cosmos is so astonishing that awe, wonder, and curiosity become its veracity. We have no option but adoration. The whole mystery of gravity and electromagnetic frequencies leave us speechless. To think that science will one day master or even have the language to describe them is obscene. The fundamental forces of life upon our planet happened in a millionth of a second, and the seed and marvellous welfare of our human family lay nascent in it. If, in the nanosecond of the Big Bang, the explosion had misfired, the universe would either flow as liquid or burn into a fireball incapable of supporting the precise habitat for human existence. We humans are placed amongst the stars on a Goldilocks planet. If Jupiter was not situated as an umbrella above us, humanity would soon be pulverised from all the meteorites, asteroids, and debris falling upon it.

Were any of the precise happenings missing in the nanosecond explosion of the Big Bang, then human life would not be possible. It would seem the Big Bang had Homo sapiens in mind from the very beginning. We have been baptised and created from stardust. When confronted by the fifty billion galaxies in our universe, how can anyone of us be so arrogant as to say the reality of our small perception can define all the incredible mystery which envelops us? Surely such a reality must conjure up wonder. Fundamentalism of any sort, whether it be religious or atheistic, must be at all costs considered outrageous. Both systems plunder wonder. Organised religion is too definite and sure of itself. It leaves no room for heresy. It fails to realise that heresy carries with it questions which can spur us on to leave behind stale answers. Heresy can be a good motivator when it stays within the parameter of reasonable behaviour. Organised religion has failed miserably in its mission to evangelise the compassion of Jesus Christ to its assembly of faith followers. This may sound like heresy to the ears of a hierarchical and dogmatic clergy. Heresy can also be prophetic and dynamic in its demand for an end to a church which only gives tired answers. A church which is too sure of its own answers is truly an oxymoron. Theism without doubt is fundamentalism. A faith which does not ask valid questions leaves no room for intuition. This applies to atheism and faith alike. Any belief system wagered through indoctrination and tyranny cannot be the emissary of freedom or truth to anyone.

The theology of an irrelevant and interpenetrative theology become meaningless unless our Christian values influence and are applied to the electromagnetically charged wave system which suffocates Silicon Valley with atheism. The niceties of distinction in the canon law of Catholic theology has little relevance in an atheistic world about to destroy the notion of God's existence. The tribalism and promotion of our tribal differences in our social religious differences must finally become the one construct in our battle against the monstrous, destructive force of atheism. A new and emergent theology informs us through quantum physics and electromagnetic frequency that our divisions are all in our heads. They are human-made and not of God. There is no separation between humanity and divinity. We are all participants in the one cosmos. We create our world through our perception. It is our minds which create our rainbow of colour and difference.

Science itself has formulated this revelation and given this message to us. We are all one. There is no separation between us. The same one consciousness envelops us as members of the one cosmos. This insight alone puts an end to Atheistic intransigence. Terribly, neither church nor state, neither religion nor secularism, neither theism nor atheism wants us to know this. Our oneness puts an end to all our differences and topples the arrogance of hubristic men, whether they be religious or atheistic. We are all heirs to the one Eden. Heaven starts where the foot falls. Whether we wear a yarmulke or a mantilla, a Muslim scarf or a Hindu turban, we are all essentially one. Our only difference is our own distinction. Even if we live culturally different lives and expressions, our value systems are basically the same. Our cultural expressions still bind us together into the one divine family. It is the terror of atheism which separates us from each other and not our cultural differences. Atheism has been silently and covertly spinning a web of power and control over the matrix of Western society. As inattentive, passive, and ignorant as we have become, we have not noticed its fascist plan to subvert and destroy our spiritual identity. If this world is ever to become emergent with a new moral compass, then we, the multivarious God-fearing citizens of earth, must recognise our commonality. The same God unites us all. The same moral code applies to each one of us. There is no difference between us. Consciousness is intolerant of separation. On this foundation alone, we can insist on a holographic perception to be communicated in not only our educational system but also in all our social constructs. Atheism has had its say. Through its huge endowment to the public educational system, it has destroyed our natural instinct for divinity and replaced it with the false God of distraction, division, decadence, and ignorance.

Divinity is our rightful inheritance. It gives us dignity and defines us. Divinity creates rather than desecrates the human family. Divinity is non-discriminatory. It is the moral fibre needed to build up human society. It is the causality and the ascendence of our mortality. It is the answer to our question. Divinity is inclusive. It is non-threatening. We find our peace through divinity. Dante said, "In his will we find our peace."

Through our spirituality, we recognise ourselves in each other. Divinity is indispensable. Without it, our world becomes enraged by the devil.

Our present matrix is gored and disturbed by the raging bull of atheism precisely because it is godless. Atheism has been very clever in its manipulation. It has covertly toppled the reality of divinity from our social and educational system on the premise of separating religion from the political forum of the state. To the uninformed mind of the human race, this appears to be the only solution to an indeterminate question. If the truth be realised, in the first instance, quantum physics is intolerant of division and separation. Even more deceptive and confusing, however, is the fact that organised religion and atheism are strange bedfellows in that they both have the same aim. Both systems are political. Both systems, within their own discipline, desire power and control over the human race. Both systems divide and are dualistic. One favours the body over the soul, and the other favours the soul over the body. Both of them refuse to acknowledge the divinity in human holography.

Homo sapiens, by their very definition, have been created divinely. Divinity is ingrained in each one of us. To avoid the connection between immanence and transcendence is to cause chaos and disharmony in our cosmos. Both atheism and organised religion, for the sake of their own discipline and fruition, have denied Homo sapiens their rightful and primary entitlement as children of God. Religion becomes a misnomer unless it is truly understood as the infusion of body and soul together. Religion is truly a misnomer when it is desecrated by the separation and division which atheism causes.

The only true Christian is the one who integrates the good news of the Christ man as his scripture. In the interest of the human race, ours must become a religionless Christianity, where instead of rules and regulations, we give witness and spiritualise the healing message of Jesus to a troubled and chaotic world. We must do this not to convert anyone to Christianity but out of the conviction that the message of Jesus is truly a compassionate way towards the reconciliation and harmonisation of the planet.

We have reached an axial turn in the history of our planet. We must now choose between atheism and theism.

Obviously because atheistic men, through their warping, intend to drive God from our primordial question, it becomes imperative we insist that life has meaning. The very restlessness of our spirits tells us this.

So terrifying is the corruption of the atheistic hidden state amongst us that instead of all our various cultural religious expressions, we people of faith join together under the same banner of divinity and proclaim our dependence on God as the most integral host for humanity. An emergent church will either walk out of its polished sanctuaries and live amongst the psychologically and physically wounded of the planet, or else as the Church has been since the Council of Nicaea in AD 425, it will continue to be a controlling institution which has lost its sense of challenge and prophesy.

Smart technology is very hazardous when humans place themselves on a pedestal higher than the halls of heaven. Humans alone of all the creatures on our planet, because of their hubristic intelligence, turn deceptively the dust of life into a heavenly utopia. Our culture has not recognised this. Atheism has coffined us without a memorial. Like it or not, contrary to all the intelligence and fine-tuning which runs through our universe, atheism too easily dismisses us. While we live in our bodies, we humans are considered commodities to be bartered and bargained, but when death divides, our bodies are useless without our egos. The wealthy atheistic elite of the world can no longer make money out of a body which has no life inside it. What a pity that atheists can make no money out of human spirituality. If they could, you can be sure they would. Because atheism has inverted all that is good about human reality, including its many professions, their greatest taboo is death itself. Our present atheistic culture finds death its greatest obstacle. If only God and death were not in the way, then the economy would be much greater. Shrewd as these atheistic elites of the new world order happen to be, they have devised cunning ways to keep the human race from thinking about death, which lies ever before each one of us. These psychopaths, who own all the mass media and control cyberspace, become the main facilitators of indoctrination and propaganda. Media and movies not only pump out violence to teach us that life is not sacred; they also distract us from the main truth of life, which is death.

If we live as Christians, death is not morbid. When properly understood, it is a release from the shackles of matter. Death is frightening, of course. It involves change, and change is always painful. We must face it. There is no reprieve from it. Atheism, through its deviousness and distractions, puts all its energy into denial and avoidance of it. However, there is a good news story which gives us direction and a happy ending, and that is the story which Jesus came to emulate and give witness to us. Life is our perception of it. From all the clues which our fine-tuned universe gives to us, the story of Christ is far more reasonable and understandable than the doom and gloom which atheism promises. Atheism pushes humanity's holography into a hellhole of negativity and emptiness.

Beauty in itself triggers wonder and topples all our arrogance. We live on a small planet which roams around the sun at the speed of 187,000 miles an hour. Our sun, on which we depend for food and energy, is but one star amongst billions in the Milky Way galaxy.

When curiosity and wonder are reified by materialism, the music of the river of life becomes muted and modified. We cannot give a definition for gravity or energy, nor are we capable of describing the spiritual experiences of the five senses. Our very containment serves to remind us of our own limitations. We are not our own satiation. We need some higher reality to give us an adequate answer to our incompleteness and inadequacy. The answer which atheism gives insults our inconsolable search for immortality. The notion of the death of God was conjured up by Western culture not for enlightenment but to more powerfully control and strip the human race of its dignity and entitlement. Atheism is fascism and enables evil to become the dominant force in our society. Through its denial of our holographic reality, it incarcerates our physical reality through the abolition of our spiritual dimension. These outrageous atheistic advocates of chance and randomness have invaded our human perception to such a degree that in a covert and incremental way, nihilism has usurped our sense of the sacred. We have become a truncated people with no moral compass to guide us. Atheism dominates our thinking process, and our belief in transcendence is considered nonsense.

The rot of atheism contaminates all our social constructs, but most outrageous of all is the damage it has caused to the moral fibre of our children's holographic growth, which is neither taught nor valued in our educational system. Parents without a murmur, through their own negligence and dumbed down perception willingly surrender their children's mindset to an atheistic, psychologically destructive, and poisonous system. As a human family, there exists amongst us millions of topics on ethics and morality which should be considered in the school schedule. What we share in common joins us as one. It is non-threatening. Morality and a value system is more important in the shaping of young minds than all the classes which only prepare us to become cogs in the wheel of industrial atheism. School is meant to be in locus parentis. But instead of solidifying the human family with the virtues of compassion and goodness like the overwhelming control which atheism has in our evolving civilisation, our schools disconnect our children from their parents and indoctrinate them to become robotic creatures without any purpose or meaning to their existence.

Evil is prevalent in this world. Our matrix oozes with it. There is evil in nature. It exists in the extremes of our weather patterns when drought scorches the planet and floods drown our habitat. Evil exists inside of each one of us through our covetousness and lust. Evil is sovereign in the human experience. It is part of God's infinite scheme of righteousness. We cannot seem to fathom that the evil reality of punishment is endemic to our sense of justice. It sounds contrary to all we have been programmed to believe. Privileges are necessarily connected to obligations. This relationship is impartial. Justice kicks in when obligations are not fulfilled. Punishment often becomes necessary to bring us back to our senses. Then God is not capable of wrath and punishment in the exercise of justice as much as mercy and forgiveness. Then the divine cannot be a prudent judge of insightfulness.

God is our one absolute and our eternal Sovereign. Even though we humans would like to reconstruct divinity according to our own anthropomorphic measurements, an integrated God will not tolerate a diminishment of his divine sovereignty. We attempt to relieve God of the burden of evil through the argument that what occurs in human nature is made possible by its opposite. The paradox of polarity rules the world. There cannot be light without the dark. There cannot be faith without doubt. There cannot be courage without cowardice. Good needs evil to define and purify it. If atheism itself has any value or morality within it, then surely it is its ability to modify and purify the tenants superstition and organised religion. Death to the small God of the uninvolved and uninterpenetrative old church is surely necessary for a newly emergent one. Death through nihilism desperately cries out for the recovery of a new atheism. Nihilism has turned Christians into cowards. We have sacrificed our direction and the course of our conscience in the name of political correctness. We have been indoctrinated to such a degree that we now believe that to be atheistic is far more sophisticated than it is to believe in our own divinity. We refuse to attend to the primordial question of life's polar paradox. We allow and tolerate the injustice and terror which atheistic science imposes on our society. At the same time, we dismiss God for his divine retribution of justice.

The argument of man's free will does not take God off the hook. Because we are made in the image of God, justice must be as much an option to the divine mind as it is in the mind of humankind. In our attempt to remove God from the reality of evil, theologians have resorted to what is called process theology, where the God of wrath and punishment in the Old Testament emerges into the compassionate Christ of the New Testament. This answer is still only partial and denies the attribute of God's immutability and omniscience. In our theological attempts to rescue the omnipotent God from lacing his sovereignty with wrath and punishment, we fail to recognise that throughout the Bible, God, in his own decree of sovereignty, is a God of judgement and justice. No matter how we try to recreate, God remains as He has always been eternally. As we live through the terror of war, natural disasters, artificial intelligence, and all the devastation which smart technology introduces to us, our only hope is that the God of goodness rather than the God of wrath and anger will have mercy on us. Atheism is a stimulant force for evil in this world. No matter how the infidels of the earth defy God, the divinity and intelligence of a higher reality will finally judge the arrogance and hubris of all upstarts who deny his existence. As atheists refused to acknowledge the oneness of the cosmos, so too will they find themselves separated without any purpose. God is in charge and is as capable of anger and wrath as he is of mercy and compassion. Sovereignty is God's Magna Carta.

Does it follow that God is unjust? Of course not! Take what God said to Moses—"I have mercy on whom I will and I show pity to whom I please. In other words, the only thing that counts is not what human beings want or try to do but the mercy of God. For in Scripture he says to Pharaoh 'It was for this I raised you up, to use you as a means of showing my power and to make my name known throughout the world.' In other words when one wants to show mercy he does and when he wants to harden hearts He does so. You will ask me; 'In that case how can God ever blame anyone, since no one can oppose his will? But what right have you a human being to cross examine God?' The pot has no right to say to the potter 'why did you make me this shape?'

Surely the potter shall do what he likes with the clay. It is surely for him to decide whether he will use a particular lump of clay to make an ordinary a special pot? Or else imagine that although God is ready to show his anger and display his power, yet he patiently puts up with the people who make him angry, however much they deserve to be destroyed. He puts up with them for the sake of those other people to whom he wants to be merciful, to whom he wants to reveal the richness of his glory, which he had prepared for this glory long ago.

—St. Paul chapter 38

In an inverted world where honest scholarship and enquiry is no longer tolerated, and where the possibility of a benign force is disqualified before it is even investigated, the power and control of atheism compels thinking and contemplative people to ask, "Is this all there is?" The constant harangue of violence and emptiness through the mass media communication system, which is attractive to the unconscious masses, remains rampant and destructive. People who become aware and contemplative, however, realise their finiteness and their limits. There are many questions still unanswered about the mystery of Homo sapiens presence on our planet. We remain perplexed about the question of human suffering and sometimes use this argument for the denial of God's existence. The main sin of atheism is that in its random and chance argument, it does not even allow us, through our suffering, to conclude that a benign God will take away all our pain and darkness from us. Despite our questions and uncertainty, this conclusion is far more soothing and comforting than the outrageous hopelessness which atheism offers. Along with the meaning which belief in God offers us, there are millions of signs in our universe which indicate a divine intelligence is operative every moment of our lives both within and without us. Despite our problems with darkness, we must cry out the gospel of oneness, truth, and beauty to a world which is almost totally devoured by an outrageous atheism, which proclaims the opposite. As in the story of Job, we need to be reminded over and over again that it is through our perception of the ordinary, we find the extraordinary.

Who is this that is obscuring my designs with his empty headed words?
Brace yourself like a fighter.
Now it is my turn to ask questions and yours to inform me,
Where were you when I laid the earth's foundations?
Tell me, since you are so well informed
who decided the dimensions of it? Do you know.?
Or who stretched the measuring line across it?
Hat supports the pillars at its bases?
Who laid its cornerstone
when all the stars of the morning were singing with joy,
and the sons of God in chorus were chanting praise?
Who pent up the sea behind closed doors
when it leapt tumultuous out of the womb?
When I wrapped it in a robe of mist
and made black clouds its swaddling band? ...

Have you ever in your life given orders to the morning
or sent the dawn to its post
telling it to grasp the edge through its edges
and shake the wicked out of it? ...
Have you journeyed all the way to the sources of the sea
or walked where the abyss is deepest?
Have you been shown the gates of death
or met the janitors of shadowland ...
Has the rain a Father
and who begets the dew drops?
—Job 38

This message from God to Job surely reminds us of our own insufficiency. We need transcendence to complete our story. Atheism has engineered the human family to such a degree that our capacity for what is noble and heroic and holographic about our integrity has been butchered from us. We cry out for meaning but choose a paradigm which only further enslaves us. The psychopaths of the new world order allow us to appreciate and marvel at the achievements of their smart technology. Wonder and appreciation are not possible without a person to incarnate them. Virtue cannot exist in the abstract. Mind and matter can never be separated. The science of quantum physics discloses the oneness of the cosmos. Atheism divides and separates the mind from the body, thereby killing our dimension of transcendence. This division has become so automatous and ubiquitous that God can no longer penetrate our being. God is our universal magnet of attraction. The mere fact that we humans exist on this planet is in itself indicative of some cause or intelligence behind our existence. That which is cannot come from that which is not. Because God is other, it remains clear that we cannot clarify the reality of the divine with certitude. The smallness of our knowing is balanced by the trust and faith we keep in the unknown. This world can save only itself from a massive dystopian onslaught when and if we attempt to make the spirituality of our species primary. When we learn to see with new eyes, our world will become turned around. Our perception will balance our pessimism with hope, our doubts will be balanced through our faith, and our sufferings solaced through our love.

Atheism thrives on money. That is the reason why it exists. It swells the coffers of the elite who have power and control over us. By stealing our dignity as creatures made in the image of God, the savagery of the psychopathic elite already controls even the amount of bread we are allowed to eat. In our day of robots and smart technology, the arrogant brokers of atheistic materialism now consider us useless eaters and of no more value than the steaks we put on our dinner plates. In the new order, which is culturally, covertly, and incrementally planned for us, our spirituality will be incised from us. Atheism causes doom and gloom. It gives us no reason to celebrate or be grateful for the privilege of living. Atheism is not an option. For the sake of the human race, atheism must be abolished as the greatest plague upon our planet. The consistent experiences of joy and sorrow colour our everyday experiences in such a way that like a see-saw, our emotions continuously shift from faith to doubt in millions of different ways. Sometime we become confused by the waves of loneliness and despair which whip our shore. At such times, our greatest prayer is to shake our fist at God and say, "It just isn't fair." It takes faith to say our greatest prayer in the midst of despair. It is easier to break into an Irish jig and dance with the angels when we have no doubt in our resolutions. Our emotions sometimes bring us to some strange places. Throughout the paradox of polarity in the assembly of our mortal lives, it is important to remember that our emotions alone do not determine our truth. Intuition and imagination, as in the case of artists and mystics, can bring us to a higher platform of wisdom and understanding than knowing. The dark night of the soul seems to be necessary for cognition. As the mystics and the poets tell us, knowing must be balanced by unknowing.

To Know or Not to Know

Is the greatest question which confronts the human condition. Agnosticism is perhaps the most understandable escape humans can make in a world controlled by the certitude of fundamentalism, be it Christian or atheism. To be certain of anything in a world filled with wonder and revelation, by its very nature, puts an end to all future disclosure. Atheism, by its very nature, is anti-science and puts an end to human curiosity. For science to remain valid, it must remain open to questioning. Though its main premise, atheism rests on mathematical rationality and precludes any discovery which differs from its own theodicy. Even if humanity is robbed of meaning and purpose through atheistic randomness, why should humanity subject itself to mere chance occurrence to explain our complexity? Why destroy the chance of faith and hope in a world which frantically desires it? Western thought is too analytical. We are not indoctrinated with truth but a perception of it. The internal music of the spheres is wasted on our ears. We have divided the observed from the observer and, through this dualistic endeavour, destroyed the possibility of a cosmotheandric-drenched universe. When intuition and imagination are excluded from honest enquiry, then science becomes not only impeded but also unnecessary.

Despite how ladened the human spirit may become through pain and suffering, it is in the nature of the human person to carry on and try again. Purpose is not so easily shaken out of us like dust from a carpet. Meaning seems to be instinctually knitted into the very fabric of our lives. Despite the Soviet Union's enterprise to eradicate the reality of the human spirit, it has silently and in an unweaponised way reappeared more strongly than ever before in the Russian mystical tradition.

> You must understand the leading Bolsheviks who took over Russia were not Russian. They hated Russians. They hated christians. Driven by ethnic hatred, they hated and tortured millions of Russians without a shred of human remorse. It cannot be overstated

Bolshevism committed the greatest human slaughter of all time. The fact that most of the world is ignorant and uncaring about this enormous crime is proof that the global media is in the hands of these perpetrators.

—Alexander Solzhenitsyn

The words of another great Russian mystical writer penned a hundred years earlier are also prophetic when he called Europe "A beautiful cemetery".

Alexander Solzhenitsyn, who is perhaps the greatest prophet of the twenty-first century, after having suffered horrifically in the Siberian Gulags of the Soviet Union, warned the Western Christian world about the enormous crime of genocide via fascism, through its indoctrination. He understood more than most of us that "the media is the message". Social engineering is consummated and attained by an obscene cabal of oligarchs who have no interest in the common people's spirituality. This arrogant band of elite atheists has replaced the power of God the Creator with a scientific, mechanised, and controlling intelligence which they call smart technology. The enormous crime of these same perpetrators, despite their culling of fifty million Christians from the face of the earth through the Bolshevik Revolution, are silently and incrementally on the same footpath to the annihilation of Christians and their belief in God once again. They have nourished the soil of their Second Coming very carefully. Instead of it being inspirational, it is now an actual reality. They have taken the eternal out of transcendence and made it a matter of immanence.

In order to advance their cause and make it the dominant reality on our planet, the idea that every one of us is made in in the image of God is reprehensible to their plan of supremacy. Atheism is their medium, and their message forms humanity's perception. And so a pop psychology and a race to what is lowest about our social construction becomes the norm. The absence of God and spirituality in the norm of our contemporary reality spells disaster for the future of Homo sapiens. Action, whether good or evil, always carries consequences with them. Surely there exists on this planet enough will and talent to counteract all the false atheistic indoctrination which inundates our politics and our media! Why don't goodwill Christians have the courage to establish a mass media communications system which inculcates the beauty, fragility, and sacredness of our planet? Why do we continue the support the designer of our clothes but ignore the designs in our planet's flowers? Why do we continue to support and become avengers in the battle between good and evil on the outside of our bodies, but we give no attention to the battle between white and red cells within our bodies? If the Church is ever to indoctrinate us with the true sense of our spirituality and dignity, then it must denounce its own petty niceties of an uninvolved theology and apply its theology to the human condition. It must be as present in our dens of iniquity as it is in the halls of heaven.

Reconciliation is the first call of spirituality; without it, there is only chaos. Christians have become a sheep without a shepherd. Despite the terrible sins of our past, awakened Christians like Dietrich Bonhoeffer, Mother Theresa, and Martin Luther King Jr knew violence does not answer or solve any of our planet's problems. Only love and compassion can address what is the deepest yearning of the human experience. The atheism of the elites is armed with weapons of deceit, smart technology, and indecency to destroy us. Our greatest tragedy is that not even the pope sounds outraged about its onslaught. As we lie passive and indifferent on our couches, Christians are covertly and incrementally being brought to the same frightful end of elimination in the United States of America as they were in the Bolshevik revolution of the Soviet Union. When the spirituality of the human person is discarded as unimportant, then atheistic communism and fascism inevitably controls a nation's moral compass. Like it or not, a hidden cabal of fascists already controls the United States. Silicon Valley has conspired to keep the common people in ignorance. Like a spider waiting at the centre of its web, while it promises comfort and convenience to uninformed flies who swarm outside, the deceitful spider prepares sticky honey threads to allure and entice us. But the sweetness is meant to devour rather than feed us. What has happened in the Soviet Union is about to repeat in the United States of America. Fascism adopts us when spirituality deserts us.

Nature itself will always have the final say. No matter the claims of atheism, it does not give us an adequate answer to our search for meaning. Nature itself can never attenuate its own destruction. With or without us, God will always be immortal and eternal. There is no other answer or resolution to our human predicament. If we humans become an extinct species on our planet during the experiment divinity has with the human family, then God in his wisdom will probably experiment with another evolutionary story. God will not end his primordial agenda of justice simply because atheism ends his plan of eternal consciousness. Like a hen who covers her little flock of chicks, he will gather those who have been faithful to their creation under his wings and start again. Divinity is eternally generative. Atheism, on the other hand, is non-creative. It is purely non-viable. The compassionate message of Jesus is clearly complementary to God's will. It will work if we allow other perceptions and atheistic creeds to allow it to succeed. Otherwise, perhaps one day human arrogance and sense of superiority shall succumb to humility. Only then shall God's operative pleasure and power be consummated.

Some say our opulence is our decay. We want freedom but not the addendum of discipline. As in all of nature, this is an impossibility. Heaven is here already; it starts with our footfall. Sadly, atheism has not allowed us to make the connection between immanence and transcendence. Atheism postulates and proposes that science alone can deliver a utopia to our search. Yet the new findings of quantum mechanics and electromagnetic frequencies point towards the possibility of a higher reality which in essence destroys the tenets of atheism. It would seem obvious even from a scientific perspective that atheistic science is its own worst enemy. Atheistic science continues the myth of its supremacy, whereas authentic science is not at all contradictory but complementary to our holographic reality. The more science unfolds the great secrets of the universe, the more its revelation of some divine cause increases. The atomic particle weaves its way into consciousness. The principle of divinity holds matter and spirit together. Unity and the underlying principle of life. However, this principle, which cannot be dismissed, is ignored by the atheism of the elite to increase the indoctrination of separation which best suits their agenda. When wars are waged for the justice of human integrity instead of money, only then can peace be attained.

The menu of choice for our future generations is already here on our dining tables. Sadly, the meat vegetables and bread of our choosing have been modified to such a degree that they are contaminated with the toxicity of atheism. The woeful reality of destruction in our everyday family lives impacts our moral compass much more than we realise. Our atheistic culture has genetically modified not only our bodies but even more dangerously our very spirits. Atheism is dangerous. It is a whitened Sepulchre. But we do not realise it. There is a rotten, stinking corpse beneath the veneer of its purity and beauty. The atheistic paradigm which the West is now designed to follow is counter-intuitive. To defeat it is obligatory. When and if this happens, as quantum physics and electromagnetic frequency tells us it must, then all the petty, unjust wars and the terrorism which America, Israel, and Europe have imposed on the world will cease. We have depleted ourselves of sensibility in favour of nonsense. Our programming is owned and propagated by atheism. Whether or not we believe in God, the established church of atheism must be toppled simply because it is not good for human society. Our very matrix tells us this. Agnostics and theists, doubters and believers must join together and become as cunning in the destruction of atheism as its leading cabal of psychopaths were in the destruction of Western Christian culture. We have been so swallowed up by the nihilism of atheism in the West and so miseducated that we are now incapable of knowing and seeing the relationship between the material and the spiritual. We have dualistically divided our holographic reality. When we kiss and love our own little children, we fail to recognise it is a kiss and a prayer we make to the transcendent reality of some higher being.

We fail to recognise that the choices we are confronted with every day, no matter how small, are related to much more enormous issues. Atheism does not want us to know that our temporality has an impact on our eternity. The common people amongst us have been indoctrinated by organised religion to think that going to church on a Sunday morning makes us holy and spiritual. This attitude inculcates nothing but avoidance and an escape from the truth which Jesus preached. Holiness comes from one's interior disposition and not through obedience to external laws. To pull a drowning animal from a flooded field on a Sunday morning is far more spiritual and human than allowing it to suffer and drown. If we were more informed spiritually, God would surely tell us that the washing of our little babies' dirty backsides pleases him much more than the rote recitation of a hundred uninvolved rosaries. The task before the social construct of this world, if it would not perish, is not only the destruction of atheism but also the holographic reconstruction of a meaningful and informed theology which will guide us to the truth. Of all the iconic heroes on our planet, Jesus of Nazareth must surely be singular amongst them. He declared in humility, "I am the way—the truth—and the life." Atheism sniffs and snorts at such a perspective and desires to vociferously destroy Christianity. Atheism has weaponised vulgarity and decadence to weaken and destroy the Christian heritage of the West. The European Union does not even mention the name of God, much less call out for divinity's direction and encouragement in its constitution.

Ordinary lower- and middle-class Americans have yet to learn that the Federal Reserve is not owned by them. Their capital and Capitol are run by a group of vultures who devour and destroy every vestige of moral value from their spirits.

Economy alone has become the content of our modern paradigm. Our perception and appreciation has been formed mostly by the indoctrination of our advertising and mass media. We have become, as a result, skim milk with all the cream separated out of us. We live in an illusory, dystopian reality which virtually separates us from the real. All the wonder of the real and natural world has been forgotten, and our human capacity for appreciation astonishment and reverence has been radically butchered out of us. It has been replaced through the manipulation of a cyborg reality. The violence, bloodletting, disrespect, decadence, and dissonance we experience in our movies and television are daily contaminating us. We have adapted to the messages of the virtual and made them a living reality in the vulgarity of our daily lives. How can a society which is pumped with an atheistic agenda become anything more that the values indoctrinated into its mindset? We gather as algae on the top of diseased water when the purity and availability of oxygen is drained out of us.

The decadence and dirt of atheism is spreading all over the Christian world. The aim of atheism is to destroy not only Christianity but also all semblances of honour and decency so that its own tribe of rich aristocrats may live as supremacists.

Instead of organised religion being prophetic in such threatening times, it has remained mute and cowardly against the awful destruction which atheism is causing in the Christian world. Ever vigilant to protect its own doctrine, it continues to preach a tired religion which misses the message of its suffering servant and wounded healer. Tidy definitions and controlling messages are no longer adequate to hunt the howling growling wolves at the door of the Christian world. If materialistic atheism succeeds, then all the glorious wisdom, literature, architecture, paintings, and music of the Christian Church will be destroyed forever. Despite the Church's Inquisition and land-grabbing, it still has been a force for Good in the world. It behoves the papacy to speak audaciously the teaching of Jesus in a more prophetic and forceful way. The message of the man from Nazareth is the most inclusive and restorative rhetoric ever to be spoken to reach the mind of humans. Our planet has not been so alarmingly threaten by artificial intelligence or smart technology, and never more than now has this world needed to emphasise that the human heart must be central to all our endeavours. Atheistically driven smart technology lures us into a fool's paradise by its promise of comfort and convenience. It does so to entrap us in such a way that finally it can control us. 5G technology has been created to radiate us. What use is any improvement and convenience which smart technology offers us when it has butchered the human heart out of life? Machines cannot feel, nor do they have love for one another. Even if artificial intelligence can create the neurology of feeling, such an accomplishment would be redundant. Why would a machine that loves be superior to a human who loves? It seems like an awful waste of energy to create such a machine. Even if it is ever manufactured, it would be only a copy of the original. Sadly, our world has become more impressed by our social engineering and machinery than we are in the miraculous machinery of nature which daily implodes without any fireworks in the midst of our ordinary world.

It is through the frequency of the human heart alone that we have the ability to appreciate anything. Atheism denies the higher frequency of God who is love. When we delete God from human affairs, we no longer have a reason to be joyful or hopeful. Without God, there is no reason for singing or dancing.

It was the Church which built the foundation for scientific investigation. Never in human history has Christianity been more threatened. The Christian Church must step up to the plate once again and save Christianity from becoming extinct in the Western world. Pope Paul has told us that we must obey the

United Nations, but does not know, or perhaps does he collude with, Agenda 21-30, which denies us the right to own private property?

If the paradigm of atheism continues to smother the human mind, then all the accomplishments of the human spirit, which Christian art gave to the world, will have its hidden symbolic meaning, subtracted from it. Atheism will turn Christian art into museum pieces. Such an art loses the disclosure of creativeness when it is removed from the living reality of its subjectivity.

The Human Body

We have seen how atheistic materialism destroys and diminishes the artistic creative genius of the human person. Contrary to the control and propaganda of our atheistic mass media, there still exists in human consciousness the spirit of resistance and resilience. This fact alone indicates that within our species, a soul exists which is far more powerful than any hideous indoctrination. Rebels and whistle-blowers are the most authentic soldiers and patriots in a society which is steeped in corruption. Along with such courageous witnessing instilled by a moral code, there are billions of other symbolic clues which give evidence and proof to the existence of a divine intelligence infusing and interfacing with our human existence.

The human body is the most precious and awe-inspiring testament of God's presence in our sensate world. Apart from the awe and wonder which the human cell invites, the mechanism and mathematical complexity of its creation staggers the mind and makes its technological sign of some astounding transcendent composition. The thirty trillion cells in the human body carry enough information in each cell to replicate the human person over thirty trillion times. Every cell carries with it enough information to duplicate an exact copy of the thirty trillion cells which are needed to create a human body. How is it possible to accomplish such a miracle of nanotechnology without falling on our knees in adoration and astonishment? Surely such a feat in engineering is due to some supreme intelligent designer! Atheism dismisses the argument of irreducible causality and the evidential beauty and power of a designer and creator, who without our awareness disposes with energy the meeting of two matrix cells to become thirty trillion dancing with life after the period of nine month's pregnancy. We stand fixated with wonder at the marvel of Jesus turning water into wine, but the miracle of two cells multiplying into thirty trillion scarcely awakens us to the miracles which happen within our own bodies. God is never more descendant and available than in the birth of a baby. In every human incarnation, he blesses the flesh of our human predicament. Resurrection is a daily occurrence in our ordinary lives, but we do not know how to convert its reality into an eternal ring of unity and consciousness. In birth we break forth from the darkness of our mothers' wombs. A death occurs in every birth. We break into a new light when we are born only to be compelled to surrender the candle of our shadowed life to the dark. The new dark is the same as the dark in our mothers' wombs. Silently without an effort on its part, it prepares us for another breaking forth from the tomb of our womb. The death of the human body is not the end. It is but the loosening of the incarnation ropes which tie us down. Death is but a release from the shackles of matter. To be born, we must leave the afterbirth plasm and the umbilical cord behind. To transcend into the divine, we must resurrect ourselves two times. The resurrection from our physical reality is complicated by our conscience and the fear of the unknown. In truth, when we understand consciousness, it is a benign reality. Just as in the first resurrection from our mothers' wombs, when we were not conscious of our own being, the same energy carries on electromagnetically within and without our death experience. Our faith tells us that a divine reality runs on eternally through all reality. Atheism tells us that death brings a closure to everything. These ministers of our new world order canonise death for the sake of their own economy. In fact, it is their own power-driven remit which causes death to be our greatest taboo.

So much is given to us, but because it is in the ordinary, we are never shocked by its beauty. We are given a pearl of great price, but we do not treasure it. We can no longer see what is essential. Millions of good tiding messages are sent to us daily, but we never open the envelope which contains them. The machines of our own bodies are such an astounding incarnation that after four million years, we still are in the infant stage of understanding their complexity. Each one of us is a creature of such profound and intricate proportion that only God could have created us.

DNA is the fundamental building block in the nucleus of each living cell. The majestic complexity of this tiny piece of reality staggers the mind. The information carried on its double spiral would fill a book of two hundred thousand pages. Each one of us is a living library. This finding of science remains unmanifest to most of us. Yet in silence it carries on its daily routine of accomplishment and determination. The incredible opening of our DNA by the Human Genome Project gives us an objective view of the inner core of the cell. Such a view in itself bespeaks a trait of some omnipresent splendour at work in the universe. This nanocreation alone must surely make all microbiologists very jealous. The great sin of atheism is that it smothers wonder and promotes boredom only to feed it with the pablum of an egoic overindulgence. Atheistic materialism creates jaded, apathetic, and listless people who have lost their ability to wonder.

Boredom is their custom, and their only relief is their effort to placate their restlessness with the empty promise of consumerism. Shopping malls are our new churches. Jaded children wonder at nothing. There has to be something rather than nothing. If this is not so, then life becomes anxiety-driven and purposeless. Even joy has no meaning.

We must ask why atheism has gained such a hold in the perception of the Christian world. Through our listless and careless attitude towards the spirituality of our own interior, we have become one with the agitator who dominates and indoctrinates us to feel and act inferiorly. It is astounding that the Christian mind, which has in the past brought so much outstanding and beautiful art into our world through the connection between immanence and transcendence, should so easily allow the arrogance of atheism to rob us of our capacity for beauty and transcendence. Despite atheism's promise of a utopian future, the fact remains that the human spirit will continue to remain restless unless and until it rests in beauty. Atheism cannot build its own eschatology on the grounds of a false economy. We are doomed to be spiritual. To become fully incarnate, our transcendent aspect must become primary. Love is our highest achievement. To find it, we must first live it. The latest gadgets from smart technology may speak back to us, but they will never love us, especially in our age of weaponised lasered, electromagnetic energy. The human race has had the wool pulled over its eyes through the indoctrination of and intent of the atheistic cabal, who are on the edge of establishing their new world order.

We no longer wonder at the facts which secular science has disclosed to us as truly factual and reliable. Life is far more mysterious and mystical than our five senses tell us. For instance, the atom, which is the most fundamental building block in matter, is over 99 per cent empty. This is a scientific fact. Our material world is practically invisible, so what we perceive is only an illusion. We have never been schooled to understand that our five senses alone give us only partial information about our earthly reality. What is deepest about the human condition lies beneath the surface. Our senses warp or at least minimise our understanding of what is real. We find it difficult to believe that matter is an illusion. Our senses tell us that materiality invades most of our space, but in reality it is as empty as is its foundational atomic reality. Emptiness is invisible. For this reason alone, we must look beyond our physicality to understand the reality of our humanity. Atheism restricts our understanding of what is real. It makes materiality primary when in fact what is deepest about the human condition goes beyond the ability of our five senses to understand. We are far more than what our five senses tell us. If atheistic fundamentalists want accuracy, then they must appreciate that what lies beneath the water surface of the iceberg is the groundswell and foundational bulk beneath it.

What really exists is inside of us; what is outside is merely what we perceive. As all of us know too well, our perceptions become our truth. We live more by our perceptions than we do by truth. That is why atheism has no respect for truth; it wants people to live by the indoctrination of its own godless perception than it does through the principles which truth gives us. The ideology of atheism is separation. It wants to divide and weaken humanity from its best instinct and intuition. It has been remarkably successful in its mission. When humanity is turned into an economic enterprise, what is best about us turns us into competers rather than cooperators. We lose our soul in the process. It is glaringly obvious that the human family is racing down to the bottom without even the slightest protest from the soul of Christendom. Churchmen and politicians alike, by their silence, encourage nothing but the dark to envelop and destroy us. Atheism is but an experiment. It has not worked. The Christian world must rise up and get rid of it before it is too late. The very emptiness of the atom stands as the greatest proof in this world that humans' materiality does not fully explain them. There is far more to existence in our human habitat than meets the eye.

The Christian West has been brought to its knees as a consequence of the Second World War. Its cries have been "never again". One would have thought we should have learned from history, but just as diabolical forces congealed to enact horrendous cruelty on innocent uninformed and unsuspecting people in the past, so these same psychopathic elites are up to their same trickery again. This same uncompromising and evil cabal who profited from the wreckage of our last world war was never disbanded or destroyed, and consequently because of their accumulated money, they are covertly and incrementally indoctrinating humanity for a far greater bloodlust which continues to dominate our spiritually disjointed and diseased mentality. The third world war is already happening in the suburbs of unconsciousness.

Witness for instance our race to the bottom. We embrace it as the norm and accept it as part of our civil progress. Despite the destruction of our innate need for transcendence, we observe there is evil in our world, but we still remain optimistic that atheistic science will, in time, erase all the social dystopia in our contemporary culture. As with every other reality which atheism has inverted, our hope has been converted to believe that randomness and chance will one day explain our happenstance rather than some supreme intelligence who created us.

Atheism deals with the here and the now. It concerns itself with our egoic needs, and because our senses are immediately attracted to what it offers, we become addicted to its offerings. Atheism plays its game in the hurling fields of the surface. Its only goal is consumerism, commodity purchase, and profit.

Atheism destroys all mystery. It takes the soul out of all mystery. It takes the song out of the bird. It takes the design and colour out of the flower. It takes the laugh of delight out of the child. It tells the hummingbird not to take nectar or shape its beak to accommodate the contour of its host's offering. Atheism tells our young children not to climb into closets and disturb their offerings. Atheism destroys curiosity and tells our noisy, endlessly questioning children to stop bothering their parents. Atheism tells the setting sun not to reflect its red light on the sea which chatters beneath it. Atheism tells a man he cannot climb Mount Everest. Atheism attempts to explain wool without even once mentioning the sheep who produced us. Atheism teaches our children that milk comes from a supermarket shelf and that bread comes from a bakery. Atheism confuses us. It is contrary and conclusive because it makes materiality alone the explanation for human existence. Atheism makes the atom, despite its emptiness, the most irreducible cause of human existence. Atheism denies the possibility of an afterlife because it proclaims nothing rationally objective has ever proved the existence of God. Atheism cannot accept that the mystery of atomic emptiness which surrounds us is itself objective and a rational proof of a presence of something more than ourselves. Atheism goes on experimenting with microbiology and is very envious but determined to displace the nanotechnology of the human cell with a more complex rendition made by the human mind.

No matter where we wander in the universe, the smallest reality which can be objectively studied is always coloured by an invisible, untouchable dimension which defies the studier to give a final answer to its composition. The macro is connected to the micro. Neither infinity nor finiteness can be separated; they remain and exist in one another. Authentic science can tolerate agnosticism, but never atheism. Agnosticism is limiting, but it is part of the unknown in every known. More and more, science and mysticism are joining together and complementing each other. When science rids itself of atheism, only then will new revelation be afforded us. The false scientific revolution which artificial intelligence, manipulated microbiology, transhumanism, and smart technology are indoctrinating us with is intolerable. In the end, it will destroy us. Science, which stays within the limits of our humanity and our space amongst the species of our plane, gives us awesome benefits. When we wander beyond these limits and lay claim to God's territory, then certainly God will become less patient with us and reign his justified wrath upon us. When Silicon Valley falls to its knees and recognises the unity and interconnection between the micro and the macro, then surely the greatest microbiologist of all will commend and bless their efforts. We are in a time of singularity. If this world is to avoid its suicide, then the atheistic scientists who have turned the mystery and the wonder of electromagnetic waves (which indicate some majestic and awful intelligence behind them) must unplug their computers. Instead of lasered electromagnetic beams, which they have devised in the form of direct energy weapons to kill us, Silicon Valley must now direct its energy to the betterment and holographic reality of the human race.

The greatest tragedy is the neglect of our own spirituality and our propensity to believe in a system which indoctrinates us to believe in nothing. Ironically, when we critically analyse the word *nothing*, spirituality like atheism points to the same end of nothingness. The nothingness of our deep spiritual reality means it is empty and therefore not a thing. God is not an object. God is the universe's primary subject. God is beyond materiality. God is spiritual and enveloped in the reality of consciousness. Quantum physics indicates this reality. Atheistic nothingness, however, has a totally different meaning. Nothingness in the atheistic sense dismisses the findings of quantum physics and electromagnetic energy. Atheism has yet to explain how it uses the findings of these scientific conclusions to deny the existence of their spiritual invisible reality.

We live more in a virtual seen world than we do in an invisible real world. The most spiritual significant aspect of our reality goes unnoticed every day. Our attention and recognition is partial at best. Yet this living, intense, and faithful reality goes on engineering our vibrance every day. We pay most of our energy to our bodies and little attention to the recognition of its complex inner intelligence. We are more than just a set of organs. If they begin to work in a disorganised way, we soon begin to change our attention from the superfluous to the profound. When our dis-ease becomes serious, perhaps for the first time in our lives, the fragility of life confronts us. Perhaps only then will we be forced to discover the great lie and negativity with which atheism indoctrinates Western civilisation.

The great teachings of the earth and the greatest proof that God lives within us come in small scrolls. When we open them and learn to understand their coded, symbolic messages, we cannot but stand in utter astonishment at their disclosure. Huge revelation from a tremendous reality is most often wrapped in the smallest shreds of papyrus. Atheism has conditioned us to believe that the material world is all there is, but if we were to reduce the materiality of our planet, it would fit into our hand as a pea and weigh about 133 million tonnes. Surely all this points to some great invisible, inventive genius. Otherwise, how can we explain it? Surely this reality cannot be explained by randomness and chance.

The Human Cell

The human cell is the most sophisticated piece of machinery in the universe. Its tiny enclosure boggles the mind. It is the smallest unit in our bodies. Though it multiplies through its two cells of initiation into a cellular identical mob, some unseen and indeterminate force of intelligence takes possession of their expansion and growing existence. Through some incomprehensible process of selection, stem cells are chosen as machines to foster and enable the ability of our sensory perception. All these mysterious happenings unfold effortlessly within the machines of our own marvellous bodies. With the exception of the mystical mind, we give little attention to the sacredness of such a disclosure. Atheism excludes science from its divine import through its subtraction of an all-consuming and transcendent intelligence at work in the cell's chemistry. The human person may dance or sing because of the life in his cellular composition, but the question remains: Where does the information held within his cells come from?

God is more likely to be attenuated by chemistry than dismissed by it. Science and spirituality complete, coordinate, cooperate, and proclaim the reality of God, though the myth of atheism still holds an iron grip on the mind of our contemporary matrix. We are more than the chemicals which support our bodies. Without God, there is no morality. Without morality, there is only chaos. Atheism poisons everything. Believe it or not, the human cell is so complex that it is like a city. Each of us carries some fifty trillion cities within us. Like the Great Wall of China, each cell within the body is surrounded by a membrane, which protects what is transported within and without it. The cell receives chemicals from outside itself and turns them into ribosomes, which it needs to mend and reproduce itself. Transport systems carry proteins to the cell. The nucleus of the cell is the command post for the mitochondria and the lysosomes, which produce the energy that breaks down the food particles that enable its growth. Within the cell is the DNA, which carries the coded instructions from the genes in every individual cell. This genetic code or blueprint gives the instruction for the way the body appears. The comparison between the computerisation of smart technology and the engineering feats of the human cell is nothing short of staggering. Instead of just knowing, we must use our imagination and intuition to understand the microbiology of the genome. Of all the inestimable clues from God in the affairs of rational, objective science, none can be more telling than the genome of the human cell. Our genome is the most powerful evidence that divinity inhabits our materiality. Through its phenomenology, heaven and earth are connected together. The supreme divinity takes up its abode in the humble home of our bodies. Shockingly, though, its miraculous mechanism is either ignored or taken for granted in an atheistic world, which refuses to understand it. When, through the internal eye of our spirituality, we cultivate a different way of seeing, the tiny reality of the human cell, which we can only see or know under the powerful enlargement of a microscope, has the potency to change the whole landscape of our cosmos. The genes in the human cell are innocent and not deterministic, as we have been schooled to think.

Through the science of epigenetics, we now know they give us the necessary information to live correctly depending on their environment. When we understand their epigenetic character, we know one of life's greatest lessons, namely that family is made from love, not blood. Our genes describe our physicality but not our personality. If I am born into a criminal family, it doesn't mean I will emerge as a criminal. Our genes do not determine our behaviour. The environment in which we live determines our behaviour. Our behaviour is determined by a reality outside of us. The way we behave is above or epi our genes. This understanding leads us to know that family is made out of love, not out of blood. There is no such a thing as bad blood. If it exists, it is our matrix which created it. If God is good and his presence reigns on earth as it is in heaven, then it behoves that God's will must be done as it is in paradise. Epigenetically, we are created as a tabula rasa. Our future contribution towards the construction or destruction of our planet depends very much on the disturbance and recreation of our consciousness. Our very genes tell us that the earth is one family. Tribal differences make no sense in terms of our cellular identity. Genes thrive in the Petri dishes of different environments, and they become epigenetic. It is the human person in his environment who determines them. The decadence of our present matrix itself indicates that we have placed the life of our genes in the wrong Petri dish. It is almost totally incomprehensible that such a small reality as the human cell has within its membrane the power to heal or destroy all of life's joy or pain, depending on the Petri dish we place it. The greatest information bequeath this world comes in a quantum package. Terribly, we have been schooled by Church and state to be ignorant of the universal import of this central knowledge.

Within the cell lies an operational and functioning colossus as big as any metropolis. It has exists and entrances with all the necessary functions of a well-organised society happening within it. It imports and exports and carries out all the requirements we have come to expect in a well-functioning community. We stand incredulous at the potency involved in the Big Bang. We find it difficult to believe that the anthropic principle was inlaid in its stardust from the very beginning. Yet here again we are confronted by the nanotechnology of microbiology and have the arrogance to attempt to improve on it through artificial intelligence and smart technology. The wealthy rich who grow corpulent through the exploitation of the poor are the real enemies of spirituality. Their tokenism in charity is nothing less than a perpetuation of their domination. Socialism or communism cannot work unless the Spirit of the Divine is inscribed within it. One would think by now that the colossus of war and bloodshed from the time when Christ walked the byways of the earth would have taught the nations of the world to cease murdering innocent civilians. It hasn't. In fact, the lethal brutality and terrorism measured out by them has gotten worse. The atheistic cabal of the new world order will never lose control over the earth so long as the ordinary people, whom they hold in slavery, continue to be ignorant of their spirituality. Atheism suits rich men's way of life. It suits their economy. The atheistic psychopaths who advocate discipline are not motivated to help the vast majority of the human race; they are interested in their own further enrichment. They invert the law of us justice and equity through the covert trickery of changing humanity's finite reality into the limitlessness of their own infinity.

Of all phenomena in this observable world, the human cell is the most marvellous creation of inventiveness. In a world which passes its time and awareness on surface reality, preoccupied with concerns of the ego and the immediate satisfaction thereof, we leave no room for the God-given dimension of our spirituality. Going to church on a Sunday morning carrying, as we often do, a shopping list of our material needs such as lipstick or milk is hardly worship. Even our distractions are but a minimalist type of prayer. Do we ever carry with us paragraphs of wonder about our divine constitution? Instead of Democrats or Republicans, do we wonder what reality may best serve what is endemic about us? Do we ever push our incarnation a little further beyond our present reality and allow it to rest a little amongst the stars! Do we ever say in complete surrender, "My God, how really great you are"? Do we stop wishing the boring experience of worship on a Sunday morning were over and done with so that we can achieve the real conundrum of our daily routine? Do we reduce our spirituality to a chore in a commodity, such as bread, which we must buy for our bodily satisfaction? Imminent concerns such as drinking and eating are a necessity and ordained by God, but our distractions are empty and deprived of any vitality unless they are connected to transcendence. God is in the ordinary chores of our everyday existence when we understand the reality of his presence. God is like the cell of our human existence: we cannot breathe, love, or urinate without his knowing and assistance. God is inside of us as a whole to its parts; that is what quantum science tells us. We are not apart but a part. Like a droplet in a sea, we cannot experience the totality of the sea around us, but we need the oxygenated energy of the water to sustain us. We miss the God of our true world not only because our five senses impress us virtually but also because both the Church and our atheistic governments have pulled blinders over our eyes. The one true, beautiful God can, as the Irish mystical poet Patrick Kavanaugh said, "be found in a cut away bog". Or even more beautifully still, "God is a pearl necklace hung around the neck of poverty." Our atheistic, material world destroys our wonder. It sucks the oxygen of that which was meant to plough the soil of the earth. More alarmingly, it chemically destroys the determination of the honey bee to pollinate the fruit tree. There exists in even the tiniest of all revelation the most harmonious and intelligent causality in the whole expanse of the universe. Atheism destroys such a connection through chance and dominance. Most destructive of all is the colossus of many so-called modern-day Christians who can no longer connect their physical existence with their transcendence. Religion becomes dead when it fails to respond in a united way regarding what quantum science and electromagnetic information is now revealing to the human condition.

Because we like St Thomas in the New Testament and cannot believe in the explosive revelation which the Big Bang and the human cell affords to us, we continue indifferently and allow technological, atheistic reasoning to usurp our minds with a false promise. God has implanted within us divinity that explains us, and because his presence is invisible, it does not mean he is not within our homes and bodies. If humanity could see the whole world in one cell of the human body, then through the filtered perception of divinity, this world would live in peace and harmony. The dualism of both the Church and atheism is the greatest curse to ever befall humanity. The human cell as the ultimate revelation of Homo sapiens has been created to hold life and death together. The human cell is unitive because God cannot be divided from himself. Because we are made in his image, we also are unitive beings. This is the only conclusion which even the mighty atom smasher of CERN can discern. If atheistic science, which propels the advancement of the God of chaos in its atomic laboratory, does not in the first instance believe in God, then why is it looking for the God particle in the first place? Its discovery, despite all the billions it has spent on its enterprise, will tell us what we already know: that good and evil exist in our world. And what if CERN, through its division, were to unleash the power of Lucifer upon the human race? The pursuit of atheistic science is taking us in the wrong direction. Its efforts to divide the cell from its holographic inception and give all of its attention to its material component will finally destroy the experience which God intended for Homo sapiens.

Because atheistic evolution restricts humanity to any emergent possibility beyond natural selection, all the divine aspects and possibility are butchered from it. The children in our schools and our future generations are indoctrinated to believe in only randomness and chance; life has no purpose. Atheism turns the end of our human story into a nightmare. Although it may be true up to its middle recount, it cannot be true in its total teleology. The other side of our atomic or cell story offers a far more integrated and hopeful story to our holography, and we can detect this clue from the very teleology of our materiality. The mere fine-tuning of the universe, far better than any objective reasoning, points to the glory of our majestic holographic appearance. The microcosm of the tiny human cell contains ten thousand books, with ten thousand pages in each book. It dances and is alive within us, with earth-shattering information which can emerge positively for the good of our civilisation. If we choose to put it in the Petri dish of the right environment, then this tiny potency of reality can move all the soldiers of the world to lay down their guns and turn their armaments into ploughshares. When we no longer choose to split the smallness of our atomic construction and choose to understand its spiritual implications, sanity and holography, then all the warships in the China Sea and the Strait of Hormuz will turn around and go home to the harbours of their origin.

Of such is the invisibility and potency of God in the smallest of all created matter. Spirituality is invisible potency. It lies beyond our human capacity to describe it. It lies latent and ubiquitous all around as long as we ignore and dismiss it. Prayer breakfasts at the White House are only a cop-out when powerful men who read from the Bible stay self-congratulatory. It is impossible to invert the power of the human cell and atom; what is written is written. Blood and screams, though unheard or unseen, drip from the tables and remain inaudible in the rooms of men who make their indifferent and callous laws to suit themselves rather than the deprived hordes of suffering humanity who roam the earth. The only thing the atheistic elite have going for them is the patience of the poor. In the exemplar of unity, which science indicates as the foundation of human existence, the wealthy Western nations who control the economy have turned this world upside down and cannot or will not save human existence from distinction so long as it supports and applauds atheism as the paradigm for our matrix. The billionaires of this world cannot have it both ways. A paradise on earth is an oxymoron. Transcendence is exclusive to the right of heaven. Money, if it has any emergent meaning, is given to us by divine authority to be shared. Jesus tells us it cannot be used for family gain or usury. Like the rest of the world, the atheistic elite must also live in austerity if they expect those they control and have power over to follow them. No one in the human family is exempt from the dictates of our human microbiology and divinity. To ignore the spirituality of our construction is to separate us from the call of unity to which the magnetism of a more profound consciousness draws us.

Surely nanotechnology and microbiology have not come into being by randomness and chance! Why has organised religion indoctrinated us with the perception that God walks among us only in the midst of a supernaturally suspended reality? Theology becomes irrelevant when it refuses to interpenetrate our present ordinary reality with the infusion of transcendence. God is not partial. God is definite. God is not divisive. God is patient and awaits a response. He does not favour heaven over earth but uses the same multicoloured wool to knit the same sweater into a beautiful garment of oneness. The cell is the unifying string which knits the multicoloured wool into the one garment. The tragedy is that both atheism and organised religion have ignored the wisdom of the string. Biblical history and smart technology are of no assistance to me today if they cannot relate, refresh, and renew my own small existence with the positive, inspiring message of string or particle theology.

We ignore the spiritual presence of silence in our daily routine. We turn its astounding achievement of its faithfulness into an entitlement. We take for granted the blessings of life contained within it. We seldom bring awareness to its presence except in its moments of misfiring and malfunctioning, and more ignorantly, we still divide the emptiness of its materiality from the nucleus of its spiritual core. A microbiology which treats the materiality involved in our holographic reality treats only our surface symptoms. Without the complement of the whole, parts will carry on in a temporary, fractured way. Our temporal physical cures can never be totally satisfied without an eternal ending which alone can bring cessation to all the murmuring on our shore. Through its negativity, atheism gives no solution or promise to human suffering. It suggests a stumbling stop-gap measure to a question which it cannot adequately measure.

It would seem from all the beauty and wonder of our external and internal phenomenology that the presence of a transcendent reality is operating in the midst of our ordinary experiences. If there is any chance or randomness involved in this operation, then surely it is better to wager on the side of a life-giving divinity than the numbness and dumbness of an atheistic and diabolic conclusion. A chance universe is not acceptable to the question which irreducible complexity brings with it. According to Fred Hoyle, an American astrophysicist, the odds against life happening by chance is about one in a million. To the human mind, that is indecipherable. Our human evolution is precise and exquisite, but the Church and our schools have not helped develop the wonder of our appearance on this planet. The very fact that our origin was born in the stars which exploded in and around us is a tremendous fact. Yet we do not stand in astonishment at this revelation. The unimaginable exquisite craftsmanship of God's primary explosion must have been inscribed with the idea of Homo sapiens within it. The humanoid from the start was meant to complement the fullness of the biosphere.

From the beginning, the supreme intelligence behind the universe seems to have prefigured us in his primordial plan. We are the species which best configures his divinity. Of all the species on earth, we humans are the first to become conscious of ourselves. We are the people who, through our logic and thinking, can dispose our minds toward an emergent process. We can also develop the will to deny it. We are the ones who can leap out of the strait by which egoic thinking binds us. We are the only creatures on earth who should know better. We are the only creatures on earth who can make the distinction between good and evil. We are the only creatures on this planet who, through our perception, can make our own heaven or our own earth. The indoctrination of atheism or organised religion does not have the right to dictate to us what our own individual decision should shape our consciousness. In fact, it is principally because they have usurped our God-given right of consciousness that our present matrix has become so intolerable. Too much insanity, deceit, and decadence turns this world into a devil. Animals or trees, plants or birds, the seas or the mountains do not disturb their evolutionary mission. They stand fully in attention to the purpose for which they were created. Unless human beings disturb or are cruel to them, they remain perfectly content with their niche in the evolutionary process. Generally, plants do not spit at us, nor do our cats and dogs put out their tongues and curse us. Subhuman creatures never use their status in the evolutionary process to establish their power or control over us. In fact, they most often use their energy to help us not only physically but also mentally. Subhuman animals are more often our allies than our enemies.

We find ourselves on a higher step of the evolutionary ladder than our lower evolutionary animal friends. While they remain part of the biosphere, we humans have climbed into what Teilhard de Chardin calls the noosphere. We are now in the mind sphere. We are now in the sphere of consciousness. We are now in the sphere of wakefulness. We are now in the sphere of awareness. We are now in the sphere of consciousness. We are now in the sphere of morality. We are now in the sphere of decision-making. We are now in the sphere of politics. We are now in the sphere of recognising the difference between evil and good. We are now in the sphere where we have thankfully become more informed through science. Its discoveries, instead of confounding atheism, have far more laudably confirmed a divine presence in all of humanity's undertakings. We are now in the sphere, despite our false indoctrination, where we possess within ourselves the ability to rise above the perennial thrust of ignorance with which both organised religion and atheism have controlled us. The awakened amongst us have learned the truth that divinity defines us. When the truth of Jesus inundates our thinking and mind processes, then the convoluted and dangerous indoctrination of atheism and organised religion are rendered useless. Atheism is harmful both in heaven and on earth. It is hopeless in every sense of the world because in its attempts to deny our spirituality, it neglects and disturbs of our holography. Though it brags about its medicinal triumphs, it is still only partial. In attending the liver or the kidney of the human person, it neglects the patient's metaphysical connection. Operations cannot be fully successful unless they are electromagnetically connected to the patient's passion for a cure and wellness.

Electromagnetic Frequency

Our planet is wired electrically, though not in the sense of poles and wires. The teeming masses in our world who have been indoctrinated to see and understand only the surface of reality find it hard to believe that a force much bigger than the obvious really substantiates and supports our daily lives. Because our five senses limit our perception of what exists outside of us, we concretise what we think we see into a three-dimensional reality. This perception, however, is of our own making. Our evolutionary process has engendered it so that we can coexist with what is seemingly obvious to our senses. In our most fundamental core, we do not interpret reality as it truly is. Essentially, we are but biological computers. We decode the information given to us through a digitalised version of reality. This version is not real. We decode first and turn its message into the truth of our perception. Our sensory perception is very limited. We drink in only about 3 per cent of the information given to us. We make the 3 per cent the totality of information given to us and decode the rest. We live with a postage-stamp mentality about the reality of our empty, invisible state in this world. We live with the larceny of our true identity.

Both Church and state have deliberately chosen to repress this knowledge. If the human race were to be informed and convinced about the reality of an invisible presence amongst us, then surely an awakened righteous army would incite a new revolutionary overthrow of the powers who control and enslave us. Energy is information. Energy is electricity. Energy has its own wisdom. Like most of the blessings in nature, it exists to assist us. Like water or oxygen, we cannot live without it. To control and detour the purpose of its run is to tamper with the purpose of its creation. We have been programmed to think that energy is limited to a physical reality. It is the product of windmills, waterwheels, solar panels, wind farms, and fossil fuels. Our understanding is as limited as the fuel these inventions are capable of carrying with it. Outside of humans' limited interference are seas of energy and intelligent distribution, which some force apart from us. These seas envelope the universe. Terribly, though, we remain ignorant and listless in our response to our use of it. Energy is all around us. Its consciousness envelops us, but because it is invisible, we do not notice it. We retard the reality of its presence by our own apathy and reduce the flow of its universal enormity to the little flow which comes out of our oil wells. We live only partially. We refuse to see or accept what is beyond our surface experiences.

The robber barons of this world who amass their wealth through the exploitation of the resources which nature affords do not destroy God in their carelessness and selfishness, but they defile him by the misuse and misdirection which he has given for noble purposes. There is a fire within energy which atheistic men use for the sake of their own economy. They refuse to see the connection between the oil and the fire that lies latent within it. Nothing is separate. Ordinary reality shows that heaven and earth are joined together in the one reality. Robber barons, through their atheism, use the fire in their oil to temporarily warm their bodies, but in the process they burn their own eternal consciousness. Even the smallest act on the face of the earth has a connection and a contribution towards our transcendence; the Big Bang teaches us this. The body is not solid. It is made of atoms, which are essentially empty space. We walk around and try to understand the illusion of solidity. We are sure the body is a physical reality. We can touch it and smell it and see it; our senses do not lie. How can what my senses tell me be an illusion? Science tells us through quantum physics that invisible consciousness is the cornerstone which supports the atom. In other words, what is beyond the capacity of microbiology explains our reality. Some profound, elusive energy is the cornerstone of life. Some invisible and intangible force energises humanity. We have been programmed to believe that this world is what we perceive it to be, but in fact the construct of our world is mostly empty of materiality. What we think we see externally is really interpreted interiorly. Our five senses lie to us. Our primary Eden lies elsewhere. Our inverted perception of this world cannot set us free because it is simply not true.

The most horrific flaw in atheistic materialism is its twisting of the strings of human existence. It makes the external our primary reality. The ego is secondary to our eternity. Consciousness is eternal. Materiality is but a temporary experience. Physical death is non-discriminatory and is the great realiser of equality. Arrogant atheistic science, which claims it can alter the primacy of this law through artificial intelligence and smart technology, may be in for a surprise. Ultimately what is considered essential can never be changed into what essentially is not. Nature has the universal in mind and will not allow the ruin of its own integrity. A house built on sand may stand for a time, but it will eventually collapse in upon itself. Empires always fall when corruption supports their inner walls. Satan prevails when God is absent from this world. Nature is never neutral; it does not tolerate a vacuum. This law applies to both our physical and divine realities. Nature is never partisan or mediocre in its establishment. Nature is adamant and clear. It always demands the certainty of consciousness in its arbitration for the harmony of the universe.

To live immortally, as atheistic science hopes to accomplish, the hereafter will become the before of the hereafter. This is a huge conundrum from which we cannot escape. Even if the vision and transformation of such a transition were ever to be realised and the privilege of immortality became a selected which only the wealthy elitist ascendency could afford, surely such an accomplishment would end up only in a prolonged mental torture by those who become drugged with an insatiable lust for material comfort and pleasures. To be reined in by the circumference of lower appetites and humanity's endless, unquenchable search for meaning would surely be a hell on earth rather than a paradise in heaven.

Despite all the accumulated wealth and profit which this world affords, it is unnatural for Homo sapiens to be entrepreneurial only for the sake of money. It is surely paradoxical that the poor and unspoiled people of the earth can so easily turn their faces to God and scream out for help in their times of horrific infliction and mental torture. In the ordinary narrative of atheism, to shake one's fist at God in such woeful circumstances would indeed seem to be the acceptable thing to do. Yet Muslim women holding their dead children in their arms who had just been murdered by bombs manufactured in Western arms factories scream out to God for such injustice. Why is it that those who possess the least material stuff in our world always bring the name of God into their daily conversations? Why is it that poor people who remain uncontaminated by Western greed and lust do not even understand the concept of entitlement? Why do the little boys and girls of a war-torn country seem to always laugh and smile before a reporter's camera? Messages of belief in a higher reality sustain them. We turn to God when all else has failed us. The response and resilience of the afflicted is surely proof in itself that our unrequited, restless search for God is written into the core of our atomization.

> How happy are you who are poor yours is the kingdom of God.
> Happy you are hungry now, you shall be satisfied.
> Happy you who weep now, you shall laugh.
> Happy are you when people hate you, drive you out, abuse you
> denounce your name as criminal on my account.
> Rejoice when the day comes and dance for joy
> for then your reward will be great in heaven.

It is surely ironic how the Muslim world can so easily pray to God and keep the inclination towards divinity as the primary focus in their belief system. Muslims still pray in their mosques. The atheistic West is so viciously prejudiced against them while proclaiming freedom of religion, yet it denounces them as backwards and ignorant. Simultaneously, however, the Christian world, with its splendid cathedrals and artwork, has kicked the idea of God out of its places of worship. Our choir lofts are empty, and our sacred music is now sung in concert halls. Our Christian places of soaring praise, reverence, and wonder have become icons of curiosity rather than living spaces for inspiration. Mystery has been shaken out of our Christian ritualisation by the propaganda of atheistic materialism. The loathsome distraction of the media has spelt the destruction of life's inner meaning. All that is left of humanity's spiritual achievement is skeletal, with no one to sing or give praise within our grand places of worship. We become impoverished when we lose the awareness of our divinity. When our matrix inverts the natural inclination of our spirit, we become ever more warped and wrapped in the blanket of terrorism. Paradoxically, it is the culture which cries out most against the onslaught of an external terrorism. That is the very same culture which created it in the first place. Unless we turn our matrix into a reality connected to the human spirit instead of a disconnected economy based on profit and money, we will never experience peace or harmony upon the face of our planet. Foreign terrorism is most often the reaction of a helpless people against a mightier power's intent to conquer and exploit them. Homeland security is only a ruse which the hidden state uses to cover up the abuse of the money they gain through exploitation.

America is becoming ever more theistic, yet the horrific sound of the twin towers crashing down could not drown out the prayers of the people. "God, no … Oh, please, God, no… Oh, God, God … God, this can't be happening … Oh, God, where are you? God, are you listening?" Perhaps for the first time since the assassination of John Kennedy, did the nation of the United States authentically express its need for divinity to guide it? Perhaps it rediscovered its heritage and looked to God as though the divine were present amongst them. Perhaps for the first time, they walked hand in hand and apologised for their government's terrorism. Perhaps for the first time, people who have been indoctrinated by an atheistic cabal who owns the media will at last understand the truth that the true terrorist lies within ourselves and our country; it was hatched and nurtured here and not over there. It is only when we become as empty as the atoms which are the building blocks of our physicality that we learn the truth of our own divinity.

The poor of the earth who call out daily in their laughter and sorrow for God's guidance and help are far closer to the heart of some supreme intelligence than all the warmongers, bank lenders, and atheistic aristocracy who have murdered innocence wherever they wander. Atheistic contamination has been amongst us for a much longer time than the coronavirus. Instead of protecting our Christian values by wearing protective gowns to save us, we have opened the front doors of our homes and invited in a far more dangerous microbe to contaminate our mental perception, and it will ultimately destroy us.

All life is interrelated and interconnected. The single, isolated life would surely be the worst type of unending torture. The very men who create this possibility would soon grow weary of this torture, reverse its capability, and return to the harmonious rule of natural law which God first ordained from the beginning of the universe. We have put the cart before the horse instead of the other way around. Atheistic materialism has capitalised on this and given all of its energy towards a materialist explanation. The work of the world's most important strategy is to reverse the inversion which atheistic materialism has dumped on our world. Science itself tells us we must change our perception from the external to the internal world of invisibility. When we live on the level of the purely physical, we miss out on the much more glorious edifice of our own interiority. Science tells us the experience given by our five senses is totally inadequate to summate our existence. It has been estimated that only 3 per cent of our human awareness is engendered while 97 per cent of our consciousness lies dormant. We see with the human eye only 5 per cent of the light afforded us. Look to the eye of the eagle or owl, and we will soon recognise the deficiency in our own sight. As for the nose, notice the measurement and development in the dog's ability to smell. Such differences surely tell us the insufficiency of our senses to fully inform us.

Atheism forces us to believe what the five senses tell us, but in fact we should recognise the inadequacy of their clarity. Atheism, through its fundamentalism, destroys human imagination and intuition. Though insightful in its own questions, it acts like a wounded puppy when its own position is threatened by valid contradictions.

Both Church and state want to keep us at this level in order to control us better. There are millions if not billions of electromagnetic bands in existence, all driven to connect with the magnets of their own frequencies. For this very reason, prayer benefits the magnet of its own frequency and brings healing, love, and comfort to the sick person or the cause for whom it is intended. If the human race were to use our electromagnetic frequencies positively as God intended, instead of as negative weaponising energy, then our incarnate world would soon find its eschatology of joy and serenity. We have never been taught in our educational system that the fundamental energy of the universe is spiritual. Our relationship with the divine is binary. Our finiteness is our infinity. It is as if the whole gravitational pull of our molecular structure is drawing us into a higher reality, and the only way to do it is together. The only way to stay together is to stay in love with each other. Separation destroys the unity of the earth. Only love and compassion allow us to recognise the divinity of the other. Love is the only reality which gives the political realm its legitimacy. Love is not induced by law or control. It has nothing to do with the might or the right of nations. It is caught. It is not taught or indoctrinated. Paradoxically, the most just regime in the world is helpless and powerless one. If Christ's message was really emulated, then all disharmony would become abandoned.

Spiritual improvement cannot happen without love, and love is antithetical to atheism. The whole evolutionary movement is emergent. If it ended with natural selection, then the need to relate to others in a loving manner would have no purpose. The natural selection of atheism ends that energy which best supports and encourages us to carry on with an emergent energy: the natural selection which atheism advocates as the reason for human existence. At best it is neutral, if not negative. An atheist who proclaims love is an oxymoron. There are men and women who claim to be atheists yet are magnificent, unselfish givers. Such people have an identity problem and a misunderstanding of the negative import of atheism. Love is always relational and transcendent. No matter the individual claim or labelling, love is always a spiritual exercise and undertaking.

The whole pull of the cosmos is to move into the territory of something more. Our spiritual experiences are energised and excited by an inner residence, resilience, and resonance which connects us to a transcendent reality. To deny this process is like asking a rock to take wing and fly into the blue heavens. The magnificent sight of an eagle taking flight into the great yonder can invoke our wonder, but the untouchable and unseen wonder of our bodies' flight into eternal consciousness is so overwhelming that it beggars belief.

Divinity invites curiosity and plays hide-and-seek with its observers. It waits as a divine child behind and beyond the next corner in our everyday existence.

We know from the science of microbiology that particles connect and bond with other particles and make atoms. But these atoms do not remain immutable and static. There is an energetic, informational urgency within them. They create new properties which are more complex and bigger than themselves. It is as if they want to be better and bigger than themselves. There is a transcendent urge built into the very fibre of their being. If we were to really understand our own atomy, we would learn that we are cellular transformations going through time every day of our lives. Our bodies go through billions of births and deaths every year of our lives. Most of our bodies will have replaced themselves within ten years of our physical existence. When we become old and wrinkled, we mourn the loss of our youthful appearance. We see a huge change when we compare photographs between then and now. We adapt day by day and utterly miss the slow and silent process of our cellular replacement. We appear older simply because our younger cells are replaced each year by photocopies of the original. Age dims our cellular activity. Our cellular patterns are determined by time.

As Christians, we believe in a deeper and more transcendent reality than the failure of our microscopic cellular system. We believe that the same non-local, intelligent, continuous presence runs through all life in the before and after our own personal cellular existence. The cells of our bodies grow tired and become less adept at adopting themselves to their physical environment. Our cellular composition goes back to the original stardust from which it was created, but the one magnificent, ubiquitous, ineffable reality of creation behind the Big Bang, as always, energises the planet. Death of the body reduces our physicality, thereby liberating us from the shackles of matter which complicated our ascendency into a higher reality. It is because we have become so fixated and indoctrinated with the secondary requirements of the ego that we have so lamentably missed out on the primary concern of our spirituality. Yet no other force on earth is more generative or creative. It is invisible, yet it holds everything together. Arrogant, materialist science tampers and abuses this energy instead of praising the presence of the divine within it.

Not only have atheistic, evil men inverted the physical river run of God's intercourse with his people, but even worse, atheistic psychologists and psychiatrists refuse to acknowledge the holographic nature of their cliental. How can a person be relieved from his or her mental pain and suffering when the part is torn from the whole? When meaning is missing, psychiatry becomes nothing more than a swansong. Contemporary psychiatry and psychology is like a nationality without a country. When we lose our sense of belonging, our longing becomes insufferable. Mental pain and addiction cannot be addressed when the healing process of our inescapable spirituality is ignored or discarded as superstition and unnecessary. Suffering that is not transformed is transmitted. Healing is not an achievement; it is an accomplishment.

The Irish poet Francis Ledwidge expressed the morass of our disconnection and ability to see the presence of God in the midst of the ordinary.

> shall I take the rainbow out of the sky
> and the moon from the well in the lane
> and break them in two and coat your eyes
> to slumber awhile again?

We have dwelt at length with the idea of the Big Bang, postulating the anthropic principle and the potency of the cell through the process of replicating itself some thirty to fifty trillion times over. We believe in these stupendous feats. We acknowledge them as facts, although we cannot understand them.

Science alone has not understood and probably never will, despite the hubris of atheistic man always trying to explain the totality of everything. We accept willingly and graciously the marvellous insights which authentic science has given us. Yet perhaps because of the false myth that science is opposed to a spiritual explanation, we remain reluctant to accept that our visible reality has its only explanation when we connect it with a transcendent reality. Atheism has capitalised on the limitation of our senses, which allows for only 3 per cent of our perception. If we can accept that the dust of the Big Bang had us in mind from the beginning, then why indeed can the membrane of the human cell not foretell a huge and more expansive prophecy about our emergent humanity? The whole idea of more coming from less boggles the human mind. Microbiology opens up a whole world of exploding configuration and wisdom which lie beneath the information of our senses gives to us. Through microbiology, we become spectators of wonders which few people on earth are ever so privileged. Amongst these wonders, the unutterably stupendous beauty of a tiny heart-shaped stem cell, already in the mode of its given life and giving pumping activity, can be observed. If we could perceive the truth of all that is occurring naturally without our assistance, then our attention and perception would surely shift from what is secondary to what we must consider primary. Atheism inverts everything; it turns our inbred spirituality inside out. We now talk about the apparent external reality of things, as though it explains all that is truthful about us. Our interior development in their most intercellular connections with the divine become ignored and neglected simply because their disclosure would destroy the perceptions with which atheism has indoctrinated us.

As organised, traditional religion, because of its dualism, loses its grip on the faithfulness of its followers, atheism, because of its dualism, totally destroys our holographic perception. Both systems because of their fundamentalism are closed genres of perception. As a consequence, the human race is left without a moral compass. Because both systems separate the body and the spirit from each other, they deny the connection between the material and the transcendental or the mortal into the immortal. Nature teaches that the immortal is in the mortal and the mortal is in the immortal. From the world of phenomenology, we notice that life and death exist in and through each other. Neither human life or human death can be fully explained outside of this entanglement of nature. Like all that exists, the polarity of opposites knits all contraries together. Transformation is always at work in the midst of our egoic and domestic needs and perceptions because they are on the level of the supernatural. Death is very much a part of life; it cannot be avoided. Buddhism instructs us to meditate on our death at least once each day.

Whereas the Church calls us to remember our mortality at the expense of our egoic pleasures, atheism calls us to forget death for the sake of our economic and convenient pleasures. Organised religion keeps death on the frontier of its communications network in order to have power and control over us. Atheism obliterates the whole message of death because it inconveniently disturbs their system of unaccountability.

An innate fear of death exists in everyone' it is stamped on the very soul of humanity. Organised religion capitalises on this fear through its advocacy. Fear is the most effective way to sway and control its own populace. The same operational scheme for control over an unconscious and dumbed-down populace exists in atheism. The atheistic order of the hidden state through their confiscation of all the earth's wealth, and the destructive distraction they cause through the control and ownership of mass media, conspiratorially lie about humanity's holographic reality. These atheistic psychopaths do not care about the reality of a heaven or hell beyond the reality their own material world. Their only concern is the exploitation and slavery of humanity for their own selfish, preposterous egos. The reality of empathy or compassion does not enter their frame of reference. Yet these narcissistically driven men who declare that rational science supports their supremacist mentality remain in total denial of the findings of quantum theory and electromagnetism that make the human race all one. There is no separation in the great oneness of the cosmos.

If there is to be any reconciliation between human beings and the universe, then all our divisions will have to be gathered together and put under the wings of God, who is the only Creator and safe harbour from the storms of our differences. The governments and nations of the world will have to acknowledge God's presence working in and through all as a binding force, if peace is ever to dawn on us. We are the only creatures on earth who are out of tune with our own species, and as a consequence, we are destroyers rather than stewards of all the subhuman species. Lip service or mere tolerance of religion is not enough. Our spiritual dimension must grab our attention. What the world needs above all else is a holographic perspective and perception. Quantum theory demands this. It is imperative that our intrinsic spirituality can no longer be avoided or atheistically excluded from the fabric of our social values in future generations. Serenity and peace amongst the nations of our world cannot occur without a holographic perspective. With a cosmic perspective, each one of us will become, despite all our baggage, an administrator of our own conscience, which tells us the difference between right and wrong.

Ultimately, it is the self being alone which will bring peace and compassion to this world. Revolution has its beginning beneath the membrane of a very small reality. We have noticed this from the perception we gained from microbiology of the human cell and the pinpoint explosion of the Big Bang. When we consider the presence of some great non-local intelligence behind the wonders of our world, then every perception becomes possible.

Our present paradigm or matrix is not working. Decadence, war, violence, and murder are erupting globally. The atheistic perspective, despite the so-called protest of some compassionate atheists, has caused the unravelling of our civilisation. What has happened in the collapse of Western civilisation has been caused primarily by an invisible bunch of atheistic psychopaths. They live at the very peak of a pyramid which reigns fear and terror on 98 per cent of the human population. When fear and terror control us, we become defunct of compassion. This is the psychological, tyrannical terror which the hidden state imposes on us.

Within our very bones, the vast majority of the human race feels there is something terribly wrong with Western civilisation. Martialism has replaced religion in our value system. But despite the improvement in our secular culture, for some indefinable reason, we still feel our longing for something more always burning holes in our satisfaction. We live in anxious times and try to insure ourselves from the worst in our external material world. At the same time, we pay no insurance or attention to the anxiety of our interior world. The stress and anxiety of our everyday world becomes ever more insidious to the degree we neglect our spiritual reality. No drug, alcohol, pornography, or pseudo-psychology program can work without a holographic perspective. Until we relate what is secondary to what is primary, all the little plans of men will remain nothing more than the sting of a mosquito on the skin of an elephant.

In our world which plans to connect artificial intelligence to the human brain, we mystically become very worried. The atheistic function of Silicon Valley doesn't seem to consider what damage it may be doing to the mind of humankind. Its psychological and neuroscience probings are not in the interest of improving the minds of humankind but to give a superior mind to robots which can better control us. Through D-wave computers, which probe below our electromagnetic capacity, Silicon Valley can already control the human mind and, just like schizophrenia, send voices to targeted individuals in order to use or control them psychologically. Mobs and targeted armies can be controlled by such weaponised signals. Incredible as it may sound, smart technology, through the weaponisation of D-wave technology, can tell a mother to skill her baby—and she will comply.

All this is happening, and we remain uninformed. The only hope for our future is our awareness about the lethal potentiality of atheistic psychopathy. When the spiritual dimension is removed from our natural holography, then things fall apart; as Yeats said, "the center no longer holds". We wish peace would prevail on earth. Our hearts are broken with the sight of innocent, frightened people with the same hearts, lungs, and livers inside of them, searching desperately to escape the terrorism which 2 per cent of the world's population has rained down on top of them. We also see innocent young men forget morality in the name of patriotism and, contrary to their natural instinct, become killers. Little do they realise that war creates a hell on earth, leaving its residue of guilt and torture in the innocence forfeited for wars of terror, which made assassins out of them. The generals in the war game who motivate soldiers to be patriotic never preach the truth to them: that the same 2 per cent of atheistic psychopaths who control the planet have indoctrinated them to kill and destroy for the cause of amassing more profit through the enterprise of warmongering.

These same psychopaths who live at the top of their evil pyramid are masterful in their attempts to destroy the souls of humans. Men go out to war like warriors on stamping horses only to become transfigured and transformed by the brutality of their experience. Men who served in duty to their call of patriotism come home shackled and broken to the point of suicide. The ones who survive cannot adapt to the civil code which prevailed before they were indoctrinated to become killers. They become mentally tortured because their memory does not serve them well. They have violated the most fundamental commandment of our species: "Thou shalt not kill". The top 2 per cent of atheistic psychopaths are experts in the arena of pseudo-psychology. Their power is so abysmal and catastrophic that they can, without waiting for a Second Coming, destroy all life on our planet. Atheism dislocates us not only physically but also spiritually.

The shill programs in the arena of world trade agreements, weather control, a solution to biological viruses, smart technology, and the internet of things are contrived by an atheistic cabal not to heal our help us but to control us. The first utopian promise of their agenda appeals to an unsuspecting mind. It solicitously grabs our attention and invites us, like moths blinded by the intrusion of light in the night, to go ever deeper into its smart grid. The weaponising of 5G technology promises to assist us in our process. One even wonders if the coronavirus which has frightened us was manufactured intentionally by this atheistic cabal to destroy all paper money and replace it with a chip for a cashless society with the power to financially control us. The ultimate plan is to replace our holographic enterprise with a chip which determines our social credit and moral behaviour.

The recapturing of our spiritual dimension is the only force in this world which can withstand this all-enveloping plan of atheistic fascism and communism.

War is always evil unless it is for self-defence. If this world would only invest some of its huge spending on humanity's spiritual existence, then we would soon have a planet more at peace with itself instead of war. If the United States spent half of its annual and seemingly continuous war budget on a life-giving cause, then the forests of the Amazon jungle would be saved in perpetuity.

Despite the indoctrination of atheism, humanity realises from its own inner core that there is a spiritual dimension to life in general. It is imperative that we recover our sense of dignity and meaning as children of God. When we begin to realise, as quantum physics indicates, that the atom, through its bottom particle, strings into and connects with infinite consciousness, then we have learned that atheistic materialism, with its chance and randomness, has no valid proof or reason to deny the eternity of our foundation, which is the all-enveloping reality of consciousness. After this discovery, it is up to us, the inhabited citizens of a material sphere, to resonate and register our lives with that indefinable consciousness. Life has a direction and meaning for and in our human experience. We are destined for eternal consciousness. The one mystery of the ineffable holds us together. Death is not an end as atheism insists. There is an afterlife, and its name is consciousness. We go on living with the primacy of our spiritual dimension. Science tells us this. It is science much more than organised religion which now proclaims the good news of our story. Consciousness gives us a sense of our own self dignity. It raises us up beyond the material. It offers to the human race a platform from which we can ascend into a realm where there is no space or time within it. The particle of the atom surrenders to the God particle of eternity at the moment of our physical death. When we internalise this principle of human physics, we are no longer threatened by the Grim Reaper.

This is the most fundamental information available to the human species in our attempt to combat the evil influence of atheism which invades our mental perception. When we begin to hear more the call of the natural world, we will recognise it as fellow travellers on the road into consciousness. We will hug it and kiss it for the instruction it gives us. We will recognise immediately that we both are sharers in the same foundation through the construction of the atom. We are not hostile or enemies to one another. That's why we cry at the murder of the beautiful trees in the jungles of the Amazon.

There are millions of messages sent to us every day from the central office of consciousness, but our electromagnetic system has not been functioning very well because it is blocked by the interference of electromagnetic atheism. Our very identification with the natural world draws us inexorably to the woods the mountains and the trees which wave at us. The waves of the sea flowing in and out resonate with our own flow between our births and deaths. There are lessons everywhere; we may not listen to their import, yet the thrust of their call calms us down. The natural world has a voice which calls us back to what is primary and essential about ourselves. We are all one with the same prevailing consciousness indwelling in every species, depending on nature's own hierarchy. We may not hear the call, but the natural world cries out for connection within its soothing stillness The one, the true, and the beautiful indelibly exists in all creation, no matter its expression.

If we are ever to reimagine God and place divinity on its throne of supremacy, then we must topple atheism and its shill promise of a utopian democracy. One small act of kindness and goodness when communicated on our atheistic mass media impresses us far more than all the reportage of violence and darkness which self-interested atheism promotes in our movies and on our television stations. A nation's psyche is fostered and shaped by the way it is programmed to think. Confronted by so much violence and evil in our world, it is time that our capability to become spiritual and reimagine God as our new paradigm. This can only happen when the communication system of atheism is questioned and challenged. In any nation which tolerates free speech, questions and unresolved problem-solving must be necessarily addressed. Truth cannot be found when lies predominate and become sovereign in a system of false journalism. Free speech is the only sovereign compass to guide us in our efforts to discover the truth. If a conspiracy of lies becomes entangled in the human experience, then the only approach to discover veracity in our search is the surrender of dominance and certainty from either perspective. Answers come out of rightful questions. This is the only way possible to find the truth. Atheism is intolerant of this process. It dominates and controls our electromagnetic means of information in such a way that its indoctrination methods become our values and cause all the chaos in our matrix. Any system which controls our electromagnetic frequencies creates its own value system.

Two per cent of the world's population own 90 per cent of wealth. This 2 per cent who have robbed the rest of the remaining 98 per cent of the world's population from their entitlement are determined, through their psychopathic lack of sympathy and compassion, to cling to their privileged position. They have cleverly manipulated and twisted the very force of consciousness which exists underneath all matter into an agenda which suits their own egotistical, selfish pursuits. This psychopathic band of atheists are the senators in a hidden state which rules our planet. It is this cabal who ultimately select the governments of the world to do their bidding. Presidents are selected—they are not elected. The vast majority of the human race rarely realises their votes have been already determined before they place their meaningless bits of paper in the ballot boxes. This bunch of atheistic elites, who have been so progressive with their evil intent to enslave humanity for the sake of their own selfish economy, have now decided to destroy even that universal spiritual pool of consciousness which envelops the universe. This cabal of atheists—who, through their ingenious indoctrination, have managed to erase the consciousness of humanity's holographic identity—have made themselves into a god we must worship. This is why we spend so much of our time preoccupied with secondary concerns. All our psalms are secular and profane without an ounce of inspiration within them. The prayer breakfasts at the White House are nothing more than whitened sepulchres akin to the ones Jesus raged against. It is within these coffined spaces that the coffins for 90 per cent of the world's population are planned and unjustly and inequitably hammered together. Self-content with their cleverness, they fly in their private jet planes to Davos and celebrate their achievement of psychopathic power and control over the human race. Power and control happens when patriarchy divests itself of empathy and compassion. When sheep have no shepherd, they can easily wander and lose their way. The indoctrination of the wealthy elite has twisted the natural instinct of our conscious shepherd to lead us as his flock into the sheepfold of consciousness. Instead of a place of contentment and rest at the end of our journey, we, the subhuman creatures of their corporate ascendency, will be considered as useless eaters who harm their plan to cull us in the name of sustainability. Agenda 21-30 preaches the same message. The Stonehenge-like Georgia Guidestones proclaim the anthem of our new world order.

Atheism has nothing but a utilitarian interest in guiding humanity; it does not provide us with a satisfactory answer to our search for meaning. Through the arrogance of smart technology and D-wave neuroscientific capability, the elite cabal of terrorists who control us have created an image of a new molten calf in the desert. We are commanded through their Noahide Laws to fall down on our knees and worship the god of their own configuration rather than the cultural God of Christians. Such is the power and control of the elites who have dumbed down our own conscience and intelligence through their cleverness. Atheism inverts all that sustains a man or a woman of conscience. Through indoctrination we are forced to believe that unless we accept the abyss of chance and randomness, the only choice left open to us is to drown in a sea with no energy or information within it.

Those who stand at the pinnacle of the economic material empire which the atheistic elite have built for themselves have little interest in the vast majority of humanity. We have become to them a commodity of usefulness in the trade wars of supply and command. Their mansions and castles of splendour have been built on the back-breaking work of slum dwellers. We forget that castles are built on pebbles just as human life is built on atoms. Connection is the glue which sticks us together. The awful flaw in the atheistic world of the elite is their dismissal of a force called consciousness envelops the cosmos which connects and unifies all living reality. No human society or organisation on earth can separate itself from the living vibrant reality of consciousness. Yet we, the vast majority of the human race, go on serving the self-anointed notion of supremacy which the psychopaths of the hidden state use to tyrannically control and manage us.

Any group such as the Illuminati will ultimately fail no matter their claim of supremacy. This will happen because of the separation and rejection of humanity's holographic composition. The psychopathic behaviour of the hidden atheistic state arises from the fact that they choose division and separation over unification. They have taken the highest place at the top of the table and left only crumbs for the rest of us.

This den of thieves, whose only value is wealth, is spiritually illiterate. They are the most dangerous terrorists on the planet. They use the tactic of fear not to illuminate the reality of death but to avoid it completely. They cover up the exterior message of its reality with green plastic mats, rouge, powder, and lipstick to hide the fundamental clay and dust of the human body. At the same time, they utilise our internalised fear of death to have power and control over us. When we give half our attention to the material aspect, our most fundamental question, then we remain steeped in ignorance. Atheism gives us but a secondary stopgap answer to the complexity involved in our primary. When our whole concern centres on the external and the material, then the mystery of our a half-told story never seems to satisfy us. There is something about us which will not end our fear of death. While atheism avoids and covers up the external aspect of death through its dualism, it cleverly capitalises on the fear which death causes in order to tyrannically control and have power over us. Fear is the tool through which the hidden state of the wealthy elite control the human race. It is this hidden cabal of atheists who defy and destroy the hidden law of God's infinite consciousness. Their diabolical indoctrination has turned this world upside down. Lucifer now reigns over our matrix. The hidden cabal of atheists care nothing about the morality of divine law so long as they collect the money to control it. Economy is their law and content. Because of their management and exploitation, the wealth of the world flows through their central banks into their already overflowing pockets. Such is the power of these so-called aristocrats that they can convince their subhuman underlings to obey and be docile towards them as if they were the latest revelation of God in our midst. Like a bunch of trained seals, we jump to their every command, and we have become so dumbed down that we are no longer aware that rather than caring for us, their ulterior motif is to cull us.

When God is missing from any of man's schemes, then humanity should question the meaning of such movements. But in any society where divinity has been obliterated from comprehension, the question of God's existence can never be considered. Through our present paradigm of atheism, we are promised through the ingenious inventions of smart technology, microbiology, 5G, and the internet of things that a new utopia of freedom has finally come to relieve us from ennui and tedium. Calamitously, though, all these tools of efficiency and comfort are meant to entrap and control us. Spiritually illiterate people are like fish and jump for the bait of the mayfly. While we may easily accept that God exists because of the loss of our loved ones, we cannot as readily admit that our present matrix is caused by a hidden state of Luciferians who want to get rid of us. These devils even now crawl about amongst us. We scarcely recognise them because they exist in the same flesh as us; they appear like us. It is their interior, however, which remains hidden from us. They are so pernicious in their business of inversion that they make their lies seem reasonable. Any argument which contradicts their hidden agenda is immediately discredited as a conspiracy theory. The word *conspiracy* in our modern connotation is considered pejorative and immediately dismissed as impossible. In fact, the suspicion and challenge which envelops it is often much closer to the truth than those who reject it.

Why are so many conspiracy theories immediately rejected as nonsense while the biggest conspiracy theory concerning Atheism's attack on God is never challenged? Why are spirit-filled men and women of concern never allowed to challenge the hidden state's atheistic indoctrination? Why must Christian families accept the new ethic which proclaims that there is no gender difference between boys and girls? If the proclamations of the new world order are so certain of their controlling message, then why are we not allowed to challenge them? To act as a rebel in a terrorist state is an act of courage, but the terrorist state considers it treason and justifiably punishable. Such a state cries out for Barabbas instead of Jesus.

We cannot possibly have a healthy and balanced world unless we knit divinity into our economy. It is through inclusion of divinity that we find a conclusion and a solution to our economic problems. God cannot be removed to the periphery of our world! Through the infusion of spirituality into our all-consuming concern for economy, the problems facing us can be made holy and holographic. Only then will inequality end. When we learn the cosmos is one, we understand that all life is connected and cannot be divided or separated. The true terrorists are the atheists who rule and control us. Their indoctrination is the most evil of all conspiracy theories. Atheism is the scourge which prevents us from reaching our holographic perception. It is much worse than the coronavirus which attacks our bodies. If we were to consider the truth contained in a conspiracy theory, then we could accept that the coronavirus was most likely commissioned by the elites of the hidden state to terrify and control us. Confronted by the threat of death, we humans instinctually run for refuge into the very arms of an economic system to comfort us. We look to our governments to help us without ever connecting the money loaned to protect us is the same money which will indebt us with some interest attached to it. Through this system, the atheistic cabal of elites ingratiate themselves to us. We feel the system will save us. Money is alluring and is a drug, but we fail to see it is toxic and terminal. Death is our destiny, and we cannot avoid it.

Life is always in a river run; our very nature breathes in conjunction and synchronisation with the trees, but we refuse to kiss them. There is a connection and interdependence between us and every living thing. We live in a pool of consciousness. We need to restore our connection to the mystical world of our innerness. This is what is needed in our corrupt matrix. Divinity defines us. This morning's news spoke about robots taking care of the elderly. To a dumbed-down populace, this pronouncement meant progress. But to those with a spiritual perspective, the announcement sounded like the doublespeak of fascism. The human heart has been replaced by a machine. How in God's name can a robot ever be compassionate? The tin and coldness of a robot will never bring comfort or solace to a dying person. No matter its sophistication, a robot can never appreciate the touch of human hand or a kiss of comfort on the cheek. A robot, even when it speaks, is always induced by some outside influence. No matter the efforts of Silicon Valley to replace the human person with technology, the singularity of its creativity is but a copy of the original. The aim of the new world order, as outlined in the Georgia Guidestones and Agenda 21-30, is to cull the human race and replace us with robots. As ever, the whole aim of atheism is to replace the primary with the secondary. When the body is separated from the soul, only evil is evident. We see this in our present matrix. A body without a spirit is not holographic. When only the ego matters, humanity shatters. We need our spiritual component to bring compassion and empathy into our electromagnetic frequency.

Energy is information. A higher source of energy than that which exists in our human experience of electromagnetic frequencies was prefigured in the Big Bang. The anthropic principle was in the mind of God from the very beginning. As with all that exists from its very beginning, God remains in us, and God is now and will always be consciousness. God has intended us to be destined for the full partnership of consciousness. God is eternal and so are we. The full embrace of consciousness gives rest to us. Consciousness is our entitlement and our homecoming. God sends out an invitation to each one of us. Divinity has created us in innocence. What we do with that innocence is up to each one of us. Out of courtesy, we should reply to this invitation. Our reply cannot be written with pen and ink. It must be written through the invisibility of the human spirit. We answer the invitation not in words but through the total surrender of our lives through the honour we give to his holy. This is the stuff of Christianity as Jesus has taught. We have had too many words and dogmas already. We must live as other Christs if God's will is to remain on earth as it is in heaven. We must become our own scripture after the heart of Jesus. This is the greatest challenge our planet faces, and there are no bullets or bombs within its mandate. What is required is to be counterculture and surrender our ways to the will of God. We must forego the entrapment of the atheistic system which promises utopia through an ever-increasing economy. At best, economy is only a partial answer to our search for meaning and purpose. Physical death destroys the very economy of atheistic materialism. Infinity cannot fit into finiteness. Eternity cannot fit into temporality. Consciousness cannot fit into randomness and chance.

God answers our spiritual and physical enquiries with little sparks of his own divinity. We know very little of the mystery which surrounds us every day. Even reluctant atheists know without admitting it that there is some force of intelligence behind the fine-tuning and magnificent design in our world.

Because of the power of indoctrination with which atheism now controls our perception, we reduce all reality to the perception of what we comprehend through the five senses. We cannot seem to understand that the reality of what we think we see is not outside. It is our perception. A mountain range or the rage of a huge seascape cannot possibly fit within the scape of the human eye. It is the mind which creates them. We live with the illusion of solidity. Our minds create our reality. When our reality is contaminated by the materiality of atheism, then we are living an illusion. Atheism reduces reality to a one-dimensional materiality. Atheism creates the illusion that what lies on the perception of the external is all that exists. Atheism, which now dominates and has power over our perception, has made us delusionary. Atheism misinforms us. It is as deceptive as the message which our five senses relay to us. Atheism destroys intuition and imagination. Atheism destroys all singing and dances because there is no spirit within it. Spirituality is the only sustainer of a good education and the release of artistic expression. If art and compassion come from the mind and heart of an atheistic composer, then it must come naturally from his interior. Spirituality is the only final definer of the divine within us. Atheists may argue all they want that morality is shaped by human convention, but the human convention of morality comes from a prior source which inspires humanity to be compassionate. Generosity is a misnomer if it is not based on compassion.

At best, the human person cannot be but a reluctant atheist, and that pushes the human race into agnosticism, which must be respected because it involves the necessary clash between faith and doubt. Opposites are necessary if free speech is to exist; that is the only way to refine our moral compass. Our spirituality refines us and always challenges us to walk more towards consciousness. Spirituality is emergent and future orientated. This is contrary to atheism, which insists that evolution has ceased with natural selection, thereby making the 2 per cent of the elitist rich who own 98 per cent of the world's wealth perceive themselves supremacists. We as a subhuman species are judged to be of no value; we have been born to serve them. Atheism has inverted reality. Because of their banking system, we can see why economics becomes their banks and controls us. The cabal of atheistic psychopaths in the hidden state has become central in the value system of our matrix. We have become coarse and vulgar in our contemporary Western culture simply because we have been indoctrinated to give up or renege on our spiritual heritage. Spirituality is far more expansive than our religious attendance at church on Sunday. Spirituality happens and is conducted in the everyday cathedral of the human heart. Spirituality is created and found in the ordinary because it is carved through our bodily attendance to transcendence. Spirituality turns the ordinary into the primary. Spirituality assists us in our perception that life is sacred. Consciousness envelops all that lives according to its own frequency. Atheism interrupts the connection we have with our subhuman species.

Consciousness is the energy which envelops all living things. The lower species have not been created for exploitation but for stewardship. Atheism turns our world into a place of darkness where violence, disrespect, murder, torture, and a predisposition for all kinds of decadence is pumped into our brains. All this is happening, and we never notice the psy-op with which atheistic propaganda has invaded our minds. Entertainment and distraction are the tools atheism uses to destroy our humanity. Our education system prepares us only for the economy instead of refining us for the sake of our deepest and primary reality. It is our spiritual reality which motivates and inspires us. Entrepreneurship, even in the sphere of economics, comes ultimately from the inspiration given through the divinity within us. We have become so inducted with the indoctrination of atheism that we forget the true source of our imagination. Atheism makes economy the content of life and strips this world of its hidden meaning; it misses the poetry and the hidden meaning of the falling autumn leaves as they leave the limbs of their tree, which gives security. To us, the falling leaves are but the decay of our bodies, but the tree which once sheltered them still stands tall. As we turn the pages in our own stories of life, information is offered to us in great abundance when we begin to spiritualise the ordinary. Atheism deals only with the surface of reality. Atheism allows us to appreciate only about 3 per cent of reality. It is only through the recognition of the spiritual realm in created reality that we can perceive the other 97 per cent of our transcendency. It is the unseen which gives full complementation to the seen, not the other way around. We see very dimly because atheism's insistent indoctrination causes our vision to become very diminished. To advance the selfishness of the atheistic 2 per cent of the world's population who control humanity, this psychopathic brood of vipers does not want us to know that there is much more to life than meets the eye. Spirituality teaches there is a deeper way of seeing.

The downtrodden people of earth must rise in rebellion. As Christians, we must assert our divine dignity. Unless we voice our disgust with our atheistic-led matrix, the inequality and injustice which the hidden cabal have caused will incrementally and covertly give them the power to annihilate and cull us. The cabal's intention is already foreclosed in the Georgia Guidestones. The way to accomplish this is through cyberspace. Robots and AI technology are about to destroy us. Only consciousness will save us. Horrifically, the arch-enemy of consciousness is the predominance of atheism.

Most of humanity has been led into a passiveness of the human spirit by the allure of comfort, convenience, and efficiency which the internet of things offers us. We have forsaken our spiritual nourishment for the sake of our bodies and egotistical desires. Because of this separation, we have become a house divided from itself. There exists in every one of us an unquenchable longing which cannot find peace, tranquillity, and rest until we recognise our holography. A body separated from its spirit will always remain ill at ease or diseased from the totality of its entity—hence all the anxiety and stress in modern society. The wrong value system has usurped our ability to understand that it is the invisible more than the visible which nature instructs us to follow. All of our subspecies brothers and sisters follow this law exactly. The only exception is humans. Atheism is akin to the leaves on the autumn tree that refuse to leave its tree of security. Atheism permits science, through its transhumanism, to confuse the natural process of reality and form a man with a pig's head. When God is missing from our invisible human interior, then all kinds of horrors and terror will destroy the innocent 98 per cent of human society, as well as the 2 per cent of atheistic elite who manufactured rather than created it.

God will always have the final word; nature itself tells us this. Why do the cherry trees or the wild flowers of the field choose to bloom in spring rather than in the darkness of winter? There is an invisible source of energy always at work beyond their seeming materiality. God hangs his gems on seemingly inconsequential things. Why are the flowers of the field and the autumn leaves on the tree so timely beautiful and telling? Surely they give us a message of our own birth and dying? Atheism removes us from nature and turns us into half creatures, so much so that our children now think milk comes from supermarket shelves. Atheism leads to a mentality of disconnection. It destroys the beautiful imagination and wonder of the children within us. Jesus was very prophetic in his message: you must become a child if you are to enter the kingdom of God.

The modern paradigm of atheistic materialism stands in total opposition to the discloser of the divine in the midst of our ordinary experiences. Atheism is dystopian. It indoctrinates us to think that the visible is all that is, but in fact it is the invisible which makes us truly human. Any surface reality is always held up by the force of gravity. A chair will fall into pieces unless there are legs under it to support us. Unless gravity kept the stars in the universe at their assigned distance, they would surely shower meteorites upon us. Our planet is so magnificently fine-tuned that there must be some great intelligence monitoring and guiding it. Gravity is the language of God speaking to us. The ineffability of God's creativity surrounds us in all our endeavours. Despite this, arrogant atheistic men have tried, through their own tiny perspective, to assert that what we see on the surface is our only reality.

Mystery is in the seen, but it necessarily leads to a higher reality. When we look at the reflection of a beautiful sunset on a lake, it triggers a sense of joy and awe within us. For this reason alone, the object of our sight intensifies our subjective experience of it. The experience of the external object becomes our interior experience of appreciation. The external experience of the object becomes, through the connection of our mind, the transmitter of our interior and invisible experience of joy. We can expand even further our sense of interiority by connecting the sun to its art of photosynthesis, without which we would have little to sustain us. There is process in the whole chain of human existence, but atheism denies our bodies and minds from climbing to a higher step on our evolutionary ladder. Beyond the noosphere or mind sphere, our spiritual and primal dimension proposes that our next step is to climb into the Christosphere. To do that, we must reimagine the sacredness of life and that we really are eternal consciousness' this is the only way to rediscover and recover the spirituality of our cosmic unity.

Atheism has turned our cosmos inside out. and it is up to all theists, no matter their cultural expression, to unite in the knowledge that consciousness is the womb of our common gestation. We are all children of the same one divine origin. It is we who must give meaning and purpose back to the universe. Randomness and chance are horrifically negative. Negativity renders our universe useless. No matter how the egoic and profit-driven atheistic maniacs try to destroy us, there remains millions of messages from some great, invisible intelligence to our planet. We can have faith and hope because of divinity's ongoing presence in the midst of the ordinary affairs in our everyday world.

How ironic that a beautiful, newborn chicken or duckling, perfectly formed with a nose, an ear, and eyes, should in time burst forth from what once seemed to our perspective a dead object called an egg. We seldom stop to contemplate the process undergone beneath the membrane of a shell. Neither do we connect the yellow yoke in the middle as a sun which gives photosynthesis and nourishment to the plasma surrounding it. God constantly speaks to us every day in the seemingly inconsequential happenings of the ordinary. As Irish spirituality teaches there is a very thin line between heaven and earth. When we learn to become spiritual, all life becomes filled with hidden treasures of God's ongoing revelation to us. Spirituality adapts humanity to the luminosity ingrained in ordinary reality. It is only when we choose to see the interface of the material with the transcendent that we can ever be peaceful and free of stress. This world of our flesh is meaningless unless we connect it with the reality of our abode in ceaseless consciousness. When we learn to be contemplative, we can mystically see the invisible in the visible. Atheism strips us of our connection to what is deepest about us. It hammers our feet to a ground which has no story to tell us. A life without mystery is a life not worth living. This is why so many of our youth are committing suicide. Atheism takes all meaning other than economics out of our perception. Twenty-three young American soldiers who have returned from war commit suicide every day. Atheism causes endless wars. Its only purpose is the economy. Wall Street and the Pentagon are in collusion and cause the suicide killings of young, innocent Americans. The true terrorist walks amongst us. It is what is inside of us which causes the screams of mothers holding their dead children in foreign lands which determines our coherence or disillusionment.

War and terror arise amongst us because we have been indoctrinated with materialistic values, which for economic reasons alone prepare us to be competitive, nationalistic, and narrow. We have been dumbed down so that the evil which exists for paradoxical reasons within each of us comes to the fore. Atheism promotes attack competition and aggression. We learn to see the other as the competitor. Spirituality, on the other hand, teaches us association and cooperation. It is the will of God that life in this world should be lived in a unified, spiritual way. Christ has told us this. He himself is the way we must follow into consciousness. It is through compassion that we find God. If we do not want to listen to the message of Jesus, then for God's sake, we should listen to the voice of quantum physics.

Atheism has indoctrinated us to believe only in the visible and not the invisible. We have been indoctrinated to reject any doctrine that is not reasonable. Because we do not directly connect with the face of God, God is therefore an illusion. We concoct God because we are cosmic orphans. This underpins the whole foundation of atheism. Apart from the theology of spirituality, the poets, the mystics, and the dreamers who indeed teach us how to appreciate a reality beyond the visible science, particularly quantum physics, have told us that what is indivisible and invisible explains our humanity. Furthermore, quantum theory teaches that the whole is bigger than the sum of its parts. In other words, there is something more than our ego and our materiality which is beyond us and enfolds us. The atheistic scientist who studies objectively in his search for an answer is himself subjective. As a result, his mind influences what he studies. Objectivity is always coloured by subjectively. Therefore, no truth can be found outside of a holographic involvement.

When we learn to contemplate our own spiritual potency, we immediately make a connection between immanence and transcendence, between the visible and the invisible. A divine presence lurks even in the potholes of our existence. Consciousness is in our trees and the lilies of the field. God is in every molecule of oxygen we inhale into our lungs. God is in the correct equation between conflagration and asphyxiation. God is in the earthworms who are the ploughers of our soil. God is in the bees who pollinate our flowers and fruit trees. God is in all the blessings we take for granted on our planet. God makes everything sacred, even our confusions, our pains, and our sorrows. Even the hawk's claws have a purpose, though we may not understand its murderous weapons. Resolutions can be found through war. Wars can teach us through their horror to never repeat them. Atheism has inverted the spirituality involved in every lesson which the nature of our spirituality affords us. Our modern atheistic paradigm is ordering our planet in the wrong direction. It is only through the presence of God living within us that we can find the courage to reverse the blow which the wealthy illuminate have planned to cull and destroy us. We have become so spiritually illiterate that we refuse to learn that the smart grid and the internet of things have not been created to give us convenience and efficiency. They are instead instruments of atheism design to incarcerate us in concentration camps. When instruments are hammered out for torture and elimination, the Holy Spirit of God flees from the minds of those men who envisioned them. What this world needs more than anything is not things which destroy us. We need to recover the power of compassion and the human heart. Things are useless unless they empower the human heart to grow ever more expansive and used as a means to enhance our holographic perspective.

We live according to the visible. This is the precise level atheism wishes us to live on. It has been very cunning and devious through its infiltration of all the social structures of modern society. Atheism is like a shepherd with his sheep, but then in the darkness of night when the shepherd falls asleep, atheism takes over the flock in order to lead it to the slaughterhouse. We too have fallen asleep. We too have become shepherds who are sheepless. We have become a people who are spiritless. We have allowed wolves to destroy us. Our matrix has taken all decency, courtesy, compassion, and respect out of us. We have allowed the spirit of God dwelling within us to become a withered plant of helplessness and emptiness. We look for sensational and supernatural theophanies as proof for God's existence. But God does not exist for our silly expectations. God does not break through the clouds in hymns of glory simply because divinity is already here amongst us, above us, around us, below us, and in us. Consciousness wraps all of us with the oneness of a divine presence.

We see only see 3 per cent of reality. This is the level atheism wants us to remain on. When we start to see mystically, the spirituality of our interiority begins to take over. Because of our wakefulness, the 97 per cent of our missed spirituality grows ever stronger and allows us to see that reality is mostly invisible. Who feeds the birds of the air? Who coats the lilies of the field? What powers the movement of our world at the rate of 178,000 miles an hour? How does the planet, every minute of its life, manage to move so faithfully and consistently from east to west? How does the moon rock like a cradle the ins and the outs of our waves on earth? Who holds the planets together at such an exact measure that we on this planet remain in the exact position for a Goldilocks existence? Who has placed Pluto as an umbrella in the exact position above us? Who had the ingenious mind to create a compassionate frequency in order to save humanity from meteorites crashing upon it? Who created a thousand million stars in the Milky Way alone? One cannot but wonder when one is confronted by the unknown. One thing for certain is that atheism has given us the wrong answer. Yet these little atheistic men of science have managed to invert the miraculous glory of the night sky into a dogma of randomness and chance.

It is the intangible and the invisible which best explains the human person who is a much more complex reality than his materiality. Atheism has done terrible damage to the evolution of the human species. By incarcerating the human mind on the level of natural selection, it chops off the invisibility of his spiritual destiny and throws it away as if it is of no consequence. Atheism refuses to acknowledge that evolution is emergent. From the Big Bang, it has always had the urgency within it to move ever forward into a higher reality. Atheism has done great harm to the evolutionary process quite simply because it is still in process toward the omega.

Atheism has impeded the process of our evolutionary journey, and because of this interruption, we now can see why and where the material affair of economy has taken the place of God in human society. God has been replaced by money. The goods in our stores tickle our fancy much more than our hunger for spirituality. Most of us, despite our Sunday school religious classes and Catholic university teachings, have but a sixth-grade mentality about our own spiritual reality. We need a new church which will disturb and challenge us to see the presence of God in our own bodies. We need an emergent church which will take us out into the woods and the fields of nature. We need a church which will connect us to what is real. Instead of learning lessons which separate us through our cultural and religious differences, let us learn from quantum physics and electromagnetic frequencies which connect our bodies to our divinity. Spirituality is the force which can save us. Only when we conjoin our body to our spirit as a continuum will our present reality become sacred. Only then will we enjoy the full complement of God's glory in a world gone insane with atheism.

We have become so spiritually illiterate that we scarcely recognise the calmness which comes over us when we walk in the woods and gaze out on the waves lapping our shore. God is whispering to us in such peaceful moments, but we fail to make the connection. If we were to connect in our large revelations, such as the birth of a baby, when we spiritualise such a marvellous happening, we would sing and dance for the rest of our lives. When we awake to the mystery in the ordinary, we become free to surrender and accept whatever suffering is sent to us. Spirituality sets us free to see our present reality with a deeper consciousness. Even the little things of life take on a new demeanour. God speaks to us mostly through invisible packages. Sometimes his tiny messages have huge consequences. Scientific biochemists have revealed much in the understanding of the human cell and disclosure of some supreme artificer in the genome project. This in itself leaves us speechless. How can we say it happened by mere chance and randomness? The greatest scientist in molecular biology will never achieve the nanotechnology with which God created the human cell. God constantly inspires us through pinpoint explosions which create worlds of inexhaustible wonders. But because of the attention we give to a materialistic and surface reality, we fail to hear God whispering to us in the midst of our disturbed consumerism.

It is paradoxical how small packages reveal a reality much more expansive than we can understand. We observe the consequences but never the deeper reality, unless it threatens us. Because we have been trained and ingrained with the atheistic view of life, it is almost impossible for us to believe in the invisible and intangible. We have lost our ability to make a connection between the visible and the invisible. We have wagered on the visible rather than the spiritual. We have allowed a small bunch of atheists to turn us into a mob of Judases. We have sold our souls for thirty shillings and now must live with the consequences. When we sell that which eternally defines us, we resort unconsciously to barbiturates to distract us from our hopelessness. We cannot seem to comprehend that consciousness envelops us. Consciousness is the invisible reality which absorbs and then dispenses all our materiality. This is what happens in the death of our bodies. It is the bodily component of our experience which is disposed of in death. But the consciousness which existed in our bodies still lives eternally. There is no acid or quick lime which can destroy it. No smart technology or the twisting of electromagnetic efficiency through direct energy weapons can destroy us.

When arrogant atheistic people separate us from our consciousness, it is they whom God will send to the pits of hell. We are not meant to serve them or give any support to maintain their self-appointed supremacy. Science tells us more about the invisibility of our destination than religion has ever communicated to us. If we are ever to bring harmony and balance into our world, then our spirit rather than the solidity of our bodies must be allowed to define us. We live in a world which is wrapped in invisibility. The cult of the atheistic 2 per cent have destroyed our mystical capability to see reality as it truly is. Already, through the evil misuse of an invisible virus, these psychopaths have not only dimmed our spirituality but also curtailed our freedom to travel and use paper money in order to take more control over us. We fail to make the connection that the fear of death always lurks in the human psyche. Atheistic materialists use this innate fear to feed an economy of their own control with the fear which a virus instils in our psyche. We become terrified by a virus which now has become our latest Grim Reaper. In fact, it is meant as an assault to eliminate the elderly, whose immune systems are already compromised.

The elite atheistic cult uses fear to control us. The reality of death and termination comes as a shock to a society which has been indoctrinated to never think about it. Smothered in all kinds of distractions and perceptive delusions, we find it impossible to adapt to the fact that our bodies are only dust. Except for the mystics and the poets, we have failed to connect both our bodies and spirits into the same holographic reality. We panic and become terrorised because of innate fear of death. We have become so insensitive about our primary reality that we have been trained to think our bodies are eternal and our spiritual dimension inconsequential. The new world order, has been tiptoeing around us like a covert tyrant for the past fifty years, but we have never noticed their inversion of body and soul. They have been building an economic empire for the last fifty years through taxation that we their slaves have given to them. The central bank in every country is but a habitat to further globalise their wealth and selfish way of life. The coronavirus is yet again another tactic to gain global control and centralise all the money of the world into one currency. The new world order's aim is to globalise the economy and then impale our spirituality into the globalisation of the same one religion. The horror of this order is that even at this moment, through the United Nations, an elite bunch of atheists have, through their system of economics, have almost won the day. They have modified our food, our water, and our air with their concoction of chemicals which God has given us for noble purposes. Control over the human body is almost complete. In the process, we have allowed the coronavirus, which in fact is little more than a biotic of little potency, to attack us. The fear surrounding it in our infodemic age makes us run in terror from its embrace. Atheism thrives on lies and misinformation. Once the panic of the first wave of misinformation hits our shore, we may settle down for a while only to be disturbed again by the tsunami of terror which the new world order has in store for us. The only freedom we can find is within us already, but through the indoctrination of atheism, which dwells only on the economics of the body, we have lost our ability to stay connected to our spirituality. Only the mystics and the poets experience it, but when it happens, wild flowers will bring gladness to the honeybees once again, and the lark will pour down plain chant on top of us from the heavens once again.

"The will of God will wallow in the habitual."

> OH unworn world enrapture me
> encapture me in a web of fabulous grass
> and eternal voices by a beach.
> Feed the gaping need of my senses
> give me ad lib to pray unselfconsciously
> for this soul needs to be honored with a new dress
> woven from blue and green things
> and arguments that cannot be proven
> —Patrick Kavanagh

> The world is charged with the grandeur
> IT will flail out like shining from shook foil
> It gathers to a greatness like the ooze of oil crushed.
> Why do men then now not notice his rod?
> Generations have trod, have trod, have trod
> and all is seared with trade, bleared smeared
> with toil and men's smudge and smell
> The soil is bare now
> Nor can foot feel being shod
> —Gerard Manley Hopkins

> Glory Be To God for Dappled Things
> For skies of couple color as a brinded cow
> for rosebuds all in a stopple upon trout that swim.

Fresh firecoal, chestnut falls, finches wings
landscapes plotted, pieced fallow and ploughed.
All things counter, original and strange
Whatever is fickle, freckled, who knows how
with swift slow, sweet sour, a dazzle dim,
that feathers forth whose beauty is past change
Praise him
—Geard Manley Hopkins

Shall I take the rainbow out of the sky
and the moon from the well in the lane
and break them in pieces
to coax your eye
to slumber a wee while again?
—Francis Ledwidge

Through the potency of our spirituality, even though we may be poor physically, we can free ourselves from the dystopian madness of atheistic materialism. When we change our perspective from our illusion that matter is not solid, then we become free from the baggage of economic concern which makes the rich more rich. We have within us the ability to replace that which is secondary with what is primary. It is only through the courage of our spirituality that we can save our planet. The cabal of atheists desire more than anything to bring into reality a new world order where one economy and one religion will rule over us. The Illuminati intend to incarnate a cashless society where the swipe of a chip will determine our social status. The Noahide Laws will replace the Ten Commandments and determine our religious affiliation. The law of Jesus will be totally eliminated. This is the future which this cabal of elitists has in store for us. We have lost our ability to be conscious of our natural spectrum of invisibility. Because we are out of tune with the indivisibility and invisibility of our own divinity, we cannot see the crawling invisibility of atheism which is about to entrap us. Huge messages are enclosed in tiny boxes. The Big Bang was God's message of love to our planet, and the coronavirus is one of the devil's responses to and rejections of his divine message. What God determined good in the beginning, atheistic men now call it bad fourteen billion year later. This is surely the first time in our four billion years of history that proud humans have defied the wisdom of the ages for the sake of a finite economy. Ultimately it is consciousness which will set us free; it lives below and around us, and it is the smallest particle of our bodies. We are destined to go internal. The coronavirus is external and remains on the plain of matter. No matter how it attempts to destroy us, it cannot exterminate our consciousness. We have been destined even before our appearance on earth to return to our beginning and belonging. Like a spawning salmon, we carry within us the seed of a new beginning. This is the psalm of a new initiation. We have been created to sing its praises.

Remember Maurya's hymn of reconciliation and acceptance in Synge's play *Riders to the Sea*, which is considered the greatest one-act play ever written? Maurya had lost her husband and five of her fine sons to the sea. Keeners came, as was the custom then, to weep and pray with Maurya after the tragedy of her lost sons and husband to the sea. There was weeping and gnashing of teeth at each funeral, but when her last son, Michael, was drowned despite all her remonstration that he not venture out on such a stormy night, Maurya spoke her final soliloquy: "Michael has a free burial in the far north by the grace of Almighty God. Bartley will have a fine coffin out of the white boards and a deep grave surely. What more can we want but that? No man at all can be living forever and we must be satisfied."

Within these few sentences lies the wisdom of our planet. Of course death is an insult to the body. Often it is the most terror-stricken experience of our lives. Often it is unacceptable and scorches our memory for the rest of our lives. At times like this, we have every reason to shake our fists at God and defy the logic of the way of divinity. Often through our pain, we are left only with despair. Even in and through these heart-wrenching moments, we realise atheism has nothing to offer us. Our departed loved ones could possibly be gone into oblivion as atheism teaches, and we, the living relatives, are left with no consolation. It is we, the living, who suffer and ache more intensely because of atheism. Consolation, compassion, empathy, faith, and hope are for the living, not the dead. When we need these virtues most in life, atheism denies this ministry to us. For this reason alone, atheism presents us with nothing but fear. It is the most virulent of all diseases. It trades the human spirit for an economy dualistically separated from the human spirit. It causes disruption and disharmony. It is the modern paradigm in which we live. We remain diseased and terrorised from the viruses through which it purposely infect us.

It is time for our world to wake up. We are led to believe that smart technology and AI will save us. Humanity, wake up! How convenient and efficient has our world become. All we must do is tap the trap.

It becomes very clear that, as Pierre Teilhard de Chardin so prophetically said, "the age of nations is past. It is time, if we would not perish to build the earth". The geoengineering of the planet which de Chardin meant is the exact opposite of the slow kill which the cult of death has planned for us. de Chardin's proposition concerns its self with our spirituality. We are at our best when we love and respect one another, when we walk in the shoes of the other, when we unite and refuse to separate ourselves from the another. Compassion is the only resolution to all our problems. Compassion is our greatest spiritual expression. Compassion erupts out of the eternal consciousness dwelling within us.

When we wave at each other through the windows of our isolated houses, we are in fact saying a prayer. We long for community. We cannot live in isolation. Through a wave of the hand, we are in reality saying, "Be gone, Satan. Your evil intent is but a stunt and an interruption to the temporality of my process into eternal consciousness." The very presence of God reeks in even the most insignificant wave of the human hand. All human passion, when energised by love, is not only a fibrated message of care for the other but also a recognition of God's unifying presence within each one of us.

We have lived too long in a world where God has been kicked out of our perception. Because this death cult of elitist, supreme persuasion desires nothing more than our elimination, how is it possible to again reimagine a God who will save us? How can we find the emergent God of our future evolutionary process? How can we shake our fists at atheistic diabolical men who insist that natural selection is the end of our evolutionary process? Why is it not possible for the human mind, through the process of spirituality, to leap into a compassionate future such as Christ lived and died for? Why is it not possible for a religionless cosmic Christ to give us a sustaining value system which will comply and satisfy our longing for an eternal resolution to our longing and confusion? Why does our paradigm of material atheism have such a hold on our human perception? For selfish reasons, the death cult has contaminated our human perception with an all-perceptive and intrusive virus.

Our only possible response to its onslaught is the rediscovery of the divine existing already within—the divine flow of our consciousness. Atheism has retarded this flow and destroyed its true destination for the sake of its own sense of supremacy. But the Omega God still is waiting us in our present noosphere to step into the indiscriminate sphere of the cosmic Christ before we reach Omega. Christ is the great icon of civilisation. So long as we follow the law of compassion which he himself lived and died for, we all can become anonymous Christ followers. It is his message more than his person which is important. His message is impregnated with a universal message of direction and love through his life and love. We are invited to make a quantum leap into a new possibility for the future of the human race; this is the process which now confronts us. It is our only response to the death cult who has unleashed the terror of the coronavirus upon us. We have been so atheistically conditioned, negatively misinformed, and removed from the process and teachings of the natural world that we have become cyborgs. We have become things. We have become a reified reality, rather than fully alive human beings. We ourselves, rather than a holographic human person, are just another application in the media world of virtual perception. Silicon Valley treats us as just another dalliance in their hubristic scheme of experimentation. They have become our latest members of a totalitarian system which is hell-bent on controlling our perception without any concern for our spirituality.

How do we find God in a world which is controlled by nihilism? How is it possible to believe God will, in the end, set straight all our crooked ways when the randomness and chance which atheism indoctrinates is all we know? Who will answer our eternal fear of never belonging? Is there no purpose to this relentless longing for some tremendous lover?

Our literal and fundamentalist understanding of the Bible is not enough. We must confront and challenge atheism full-on. We must expose it as the greatest of all conspiracy theories. It is composed of nothing but deceit. Although it claims evidence as proof, atheism violates its own premise through its subjectivity. One cannot examine objectivity except through subjectivity. Matter changes when we observe it. We colour everything by our observance of it. We cannot be observers without first being participators: "That which you have will save you if you bring it forth from yourselves. That which you do not have within you will kill you, if you do not have it within you" (Gospel of Thomas 21).

Atheism has fooled us into thinking that if you cannot measure something, it does not exist. Furthermore, while atheism demands the verification of scientific study as proof, it denies the findings of quantum physics which proclaims the invisibility of consciousness as the bedrock of sentient existence. God is the quantum essence. Our body is process into consciousness without a beginning or an end. Consciousness is what precedes us and exceeds us. We are part of eternal consciousness. The invisible sphere of our present reality continues even though the visible container which held it has decayed and rusted. That is the way of mortal life, and it behoves us to have the wisdom to accept it. The greatest truth in life is its emptiness and invisibility. All that is without us is what is within us. The very dance of life belongs to an underlying field of energy.

> When we understand us, our consciousness,
> we also understand the universe
> and the separation disappears
> —Amit Goswami

In and beyond the human body, there is an energy which connects us to all other sentient beings. We live holographically in a unified field of a collective consciousness. We are united by a field of energy that suffuses and envelops the cosmos. We are a synchronised people who connect instantly through our sentience without the interruption of space or time. Our prayers reach their destination as we say them. Quantum physics tells us we are not limited to what our bodies can accomplish. As a matter of fact, we cannot accomplish anything without the spirit of our willingness to accomplish it. We must will our achievements. Sin happens when our achievements demean our possibilities. By thinking either positively or negatively, we send an information energy out to our collective reality. Atheism is negative, and that is why it is so dangerous: it damages our matrix.

Science itself tells us that the material now of our existence is not all there is. Yet the atheistic death cult finds its reference to kill most of the human race based on the reality of our thingness rather than our holographic reality. Of course, all atheists are not killers, but when the equation of the good is not brought into consideration, then injustice follows. Religion, just like atheism, can heap horrendous injustice on the world, and indeed atheism continues to do so as is evident from our present matrix. When the reality of our holistic spirituality comes to the fore, then war will be no more. A country may call itself religious, but that does not mean it is spiritual. A country which is perpetually at war cannot be blessed by God. Spirituality rather than religion is the designator of a nation's goodness. Cooperation and assistance rather than sanctions is the hallmark of a great nation.

Atheism is the root cause of narcissism. It separates and divides. It creates chaos through war and destruction. Mission accomplished, but the prospect of profit now enters the project through rebuilding the structure which the conflict had already destroyed. Most people in this world cry out for peace and harmony in our world, but the atheistic 2 per cent cabal at the top of society who deem themselves supremacist fascists will not allow this to happen simply because the very heart and compassion of humanity is anti-economics. We need a new paradigm. It is time for the human race to incartcarate non-violently this diabolical death cult which denies us our holographic spiritual identity.

Without God, there can be no rhyme or reason in this world.

We live in a time of disenchantment. We have lost our connection with the invisible. Atheism has covertly and incrementally indoctrinated us to follow the trumpet blasts of celebrity. Hollywood is now our global neighbourhood. It is source of our latest theophanies. Wars and violence grip our interest far sooner than the beatitudes of Jesus.

We have outlined in detail the failure of atheistic materialism to bring us the promise of heaven on earth. Indeed, it has given us the exact reverse. It has manhandled the human mind through its arrogant audacity and smart technocracy. It has invaded our privacy, and without our permission, it aims to take our human rights away from us. The coronavirus, like all other poisons, specifically attacks the weak and those who are most compromised. It targets the elderly and those who suffer from a long illness. Because it is so easily transmitted, the death cult of the new world order, whose aim is a cashless society and a one-world economy, has terrorised most of humanity through a false indoctrination of separateness and isolation. The coronavirus is a hoax. Like the weather control issue which the 2 per cent death cult uses to control and frighten us, so also is the coronavirus used to frighten us into submission. We have followed their instructions like sheep to a slaughterhouse. The truth of the matter is that most people on earth, especially the young, have within their immune systems the power to overcome most of the poison. The colossal sadness surrounding the coronavirus is that it is targeted at the elderly and those whose immunity is compromised. There can be no empathy for those who cripple a global order for a one-world economy. A total manipulation of the human psyche is already happening in our midst. We are so dumbed down and despiritualised by the dualism of atheism that we no longer have the spirit to overcome its indoctrination. The fabulously wealthy Atheistic supremacists who control 98 per cent of the human race have planned to cull most of us simply because we did not pass the test for the more efficient economy of the new world order.

A connection between coronavirus and the convenience of smart technology is glaringly obvious. Incrementally, like a flock of cattle, we have been fed with the diet of a fake utopia, when in truth we are deemed no more than the marbled steaks placed on their countertops. Like the Phoenician woman in the Gospel of Jesus, we are the dogs who plea for the crumbs which fall from their tables.

Agenda 21-30 of the United Nations and the Agenda chiselled out on the Georgia Guidestones interconnect with the vision of the new world order. Through the coronavirus, we have entered into a post-democratic era. The human race has been sacrificed on a table of greed for the sake of a one-world economy. A totalitarian grip by a supremacist death cult has taken another covert, incremental strep to eliminate most of the human race.

Soon we will awaken to the fact that the real terrorism which the coronavirus has heaped upon us is a means to destroy all small businesses and human enterprises. Millions will become unemployed as a consequence. The one-world global economy will then become incarnated out of necessity. Coronavirus is targeted to kill the elderly along with those whose immunity is compromised because of a long-term illness. The coronavirus has been deceitfully used to push the human race into a colossal mind change. A one-world economy awaits us. Through technology and AI, we will be led into a smart grid. Our lives will be lived according to the social credits we earn in our digitalised world of control. Upon entering the smart grid, we will receive a universal wage if we live according to the rules which the new world order has tyrannically imposed on us. This system of control has already been introduced in China.

The collapse of our present economic world system has been planned long before the coronavirus was ever activated. Its incarnation began when all the manufacturing industrialisation of the West was sent to China. China now makes most of the pharmaceuticals in the world, and the United States depends on China for 78 per cent of its medicine. Because China is now ahead of the coronavirus curve, it will become the greatest trade dealer in the world and, through its sales, become rich enough to buy huge tracts of real estate in other lands. The 2 per cent of the world's rich do not care about the sovereignty of nations, and that is why they want a global economy. Who better to accomplish this than a totalitarian China?

Atheism leads to totalitarianism. Unless the 98 per cent useless eaters of the world wake up to their own consciousness, the wealthy 2 per cent will have immediate and constant control over us through cyberspace. Conventional war is already passé. The great war of the future will be waged invisibly. It is up to each of us to decide which side of the conflict we are on. Will it be the invisibility of the matter or the invisibility of our spirituality? Are we just our bodies, or are we eternal consciousness? Quantum physics and electromagnetic information indicate that we are spiritual by nature; we are almost 99.999999 per cent full of emptiness, and in a world gone mad with the atheism of the rich 2 per cent, we are brainwashed to think a decimal or digitalised 1 per cent totally defines us.

We need to reclaim what we have been deprived of through atheism. In order to do that, considering the state of our matrix, we must become, as Christ has warned, "as wise as serpents and as gentle as doves". We are back in the catacombs again. An emergent Church is needed to free us not only from the scourge of atheism but also from the tyranny of organised religion. An emergent Church has it work cut out for it. Not only must it oppose the atheism of materialism and the diabolical psychological control it has over humanity, but even more courageously, it must topple the wealthy 2 per cent who have savaged the rest of humanity with their usury. Quantum physics teaches us that the cosmos is one. "As it is in heaven, so shall it be on earth … thy will be done … as the father is in me, so I am in you … love your neighbor … as yourself … do unto others as you would have them to do unto you … as the Father has sent me … so

I am sending you … blessed are the poor they shall see the face of God … when you make the two into one, then you will enter the kingdom of God … for this reason I say if one is whole one will be filled with light, but if one is divided, one will be filled with darkness."

Spirituality is the experience of wonder. Spirituality empowers. Spirituality enables. Through spirituality, we awaken from a half-lived life. Through spirituality, we rinse our eyes. We awaken. We arise. We begin to walk on our original ground. We begin to recognise an inner radiance running through everything. We see the created world as a love letter from God. When we experience this radiance, we become enraptured and enlarged. We become more alive to the extent that we spiritualise what is deepest within us. A jaded man wonders little. In a world bulging with wonder, atheistic men lead dull lives tarnished with trivia.

> This world is too much with us; late and soon
> getting and spending, we lay waste our powers.
> Little we see in nature is ours;
> We have given our hearts away; a sordid boom!
> This sea that bears her bosom to the moon;
> the winds that will be howling at all hours
> and are upgathered now like sleeping flowers
> for this, for everything, we are out of tune
> it moves us not, Great God.
> —William Wordsworth

To be spiritual is to contemplate. Spirituality is mindfulness. Spirituality involves taking a long loving look at reality. We humans live mysteriously on the edge of an expanding universe which embraces at least four billion galaxies. Ours is the privilege that the universe outside of the self is ablaze with a radiant glory in a dance of mysterious consciousness. More astonishing still is that same dance resides within the body of every human being on earth. Each one of us is a universe. So much is so little, and so little is so much.

The first nanosecond of the Big Bang is remarkably similar to the splitting of the fertilised cell. The multiplication of the cells in the womb is remarkably similar to the explosion of supernovas in the heavenly sphere. The behaviour of the heavens is analogously duplicated in the womb.

We are each one of us a heaven brought low! To the awakened person, we are left staggering in surprise at the complex achievement of the cells in our bodies.

A caged bird can never be understood. It needs to fly and sing for its own authenticity Scientific special location and objectivity are impossible when life is taken out of the scrutiny or experimentation. Full physical disclosure is not the end but the beginning of further questioning. We may know the chemistry of the water and the jagged rocks which oxygenate it, but we cannot measure the river run unless it flows with some inspiring source which invisibly says goodbye to us. If we take movement from water, it become putrid and stagnant. Living is singing, and singing is living. All of the sophisticated wizardry in our world of smart technology and artificial intelligence is merely imitative and derivative. Mysteries solved uncover millions of others of a much more complex and awesome wonder. Spirituality concerns itself with mystery and surrendering to the unknowability of the hidden unknown. Living is a carving from the unknown into the known. True living is trusting more than it is certain. Atheism is certain in its conclusion. It leaves no room for purification or questions. It already has the answer to the human dilemma before it even examines it. Faith and hope are the exact opposite. They grapple with the inexhaustible unknown and live with intimations of beauty and oneness of nature as a signature of God's presence amongst us.

All the grand luxuries in our homes are really an illusion. Each one of us is a biological computer. We interpret what we see on the screen of our world as real, but in reality it is our perception which puts flesh on our bones. What we think we see is just as virtual as what we perceive on our televisions. Substantially, we are as empty as the building blocks of our atoms which support and contain us. This world erupts out of nowhere. It is our computer brain which makes our now here. This material world is essentially spiritual and invisible. By staying with our misperception, we remain on the surface. We must use our imagination wonder and intuition to unlock the door which hinders us from the perception of our dignity and worth as a child of God. When recognise we are already living in emptiness, then we will learn it is our spirits more than our bodies which define us.

Empty space surrounds us. It is our closest companion. It envelops us. It surrounds us. It is within us and outside of us. It is closer to us than our spouses or children. Empty space is participatory. Empty space is our consciousness. It is the beginning and end of our story. It is our very in invisible definition. Its presence stays with us in our sleeping and our wakefulness. All our living is done in emptiness. Empty space makes way for our way, our emptiness is our spirituality. It gives us our divine identity. It is preparatory and anticipatory. If we could roll the nuclei of atomic matter into a ball as big as a pea, it would weigh 133 million tonnes. Emptiness is the container and the containment of all our laughter, our songs, our tears, our sorrows, and our dreams. If what is, is empty, then why is atheism allowed to deny and destroy our consciousness? If the Big Bang can, from a pinpoint, create a universe of stars beyond our knowing, then who are we to deny the potency of the mustard seed? Because the great all is emptiness, why cannot life come out of the prick of a seed and carry forth within it a universe of new possibilities? Emptiness pre-exists presence.

We are tied down too much by anthropocentrism. The badge of wisdom in our present matrix reduces everything to what is measurable and observable. We fail to see that the emptiness and nothingness of consciousness lies beyond human measurement. Beyond the last particle of matter, there is only string which connects invisibly with the immateriality of a spiritual reality. The one spirituality of consciousness runs through all sentient life. Death leaves the body behind, but the immaterial emptiness of the spirit lives on. Spirit continues its process into Omega. We do not have the mind to see or touch the intangible and the invisible, but the good in our world gives us the message that the best is yet to be.

The swirling subatomic world is an experience of unrevealed information eternally available in an inexhaustible library of consciousness.

> The universe is incessantly, even if imperceptibly, constantly emerging
> a little farther above nothingness
> —Pierre Teilhard de Chardin

The Big Bang generated the universe so precisely that our planet had only one quadrillionth of a 1 per cent chance margin of error to be so precisely placed.

> If the rate of the universe's expansion,
> one second after the big bang had been smaller
> by even one part in a hundred thousand million million
> the universe would have collapsed in a fireball
> —Stephen Hawking

The explosion of the first supernova was incomprehensibly exact and precise. Our plant in time emerged in a Goldilocks position. It had to delicately carve a safe path through minefields of catastrophic danger.

Jupiter and Saturn, our planetary neighbours, are faithful to their orbit act as cosmic vacuum cleaners, ingesting asteroids and meteorites as umbrellas to save us.

The moon's size is perfect in its stabilisation calculations. Through its gravitational pull, the earth spins exactly on its axis without tilting destructively towards the sun.

Surely such precision cannot be explained by chance and randomness!

> The long sequence of improbable events transpired in
> the right way, to bring forth our existence
> as if we had won a million dollar lottery
> a million times in a row
> —Robert Maeye

Everything that exists, whether it be material or spiritual, is permeated and energised by the same primal reality. The Alpha light burns in all living things. The Alpha chip holds still stories untold. A seed is not about what is but what can be! It is more preparatory and anticipatory than it is a presence.

At the heart of the universe, there is one seed. It is packaged fantastically. Within its membrane lies the essence of all living things. It gives our planet all the necessary information, direction, and purpose. It proclaims the hidden unmanifest.

> The information necessary to specify
> the one thousand million organisms
> that have ever existed on planet earth
> could be easily held in a teaspoon
> —G. G. Simpson

The information which specifies the complex unit of the human body weighs less than a few thousand millionths of a gram. Plant a tulip bulb, and a daffodil will not bloom from it. Plant a daffodil bulb, and a tulip will not bloom from it. Neither does a baby duck hatch out of a hen's egg. The information given to this world is perfectly tuned to the target of its receiver. Everything stands on its own electromagnetic wavelength. It is only ignorant, meddling humans who try to manipulate Gods plan and cause chaos for their own advantage. To laser electromagnetic frequency into direct energy is the work of the devil. To insert the seed of a human into the fallopian tube of a pig as scientists do in transhumanism is a sin that is unforgivable. It is tyrannical and sinful to push electromagnetic information towards a platform to which it does not naturally belong. God is the great informer, and he does not require the hubris of man to alter his plan. The Arctic fox adapts to his winter landscape by surrendering his coloured summer coat. Who gave this animal its intelligence? Atheists say evolution is the answer, but for intelligence to exist, it has to be irreducible. Something more than chance and randomness is needed to explain the universe. Information resides in the void of emptiness. A cacophony of arrangements is magnificently hammered out in the world of the unmanifest. Only spirituality awakens us to the design and the beauty which surrounds us. A boom is consequent upon a deliberate enterprise energised by information. We receive information more by its traces than its presence. It weaves into one all the mathematical patterns of the universe. We are informed and God is the informer. All that is indicates an invisible organising principle. We share in the one unmanifest light.

> There lives the dearest freshness deep down in things.
> I thought how sadly beauty of inscape is unknown
> and buried away from people
> and yet how near at hand it is, if we had eyes to see it
> and it could be called out everywhere once again
> —Gerard Manley Hopkins

Mystery of the Ordinary

An emergent Church cannot be led by the remnants of a medieval culture. We have been far too programmed by our atheistic paradigm. We have been trained to perceive up is down and the inside is the outside. Subliminally, we have become terrified. We have been trained to think that we can buy security when in fact we unconsciously know death itself teaches us that it is insecurity which is our greatest wisdom and that the illusion which the materialistic atheist world gives us is a lie. Atheistic materialism brutalises us. Its whole preoccupation centres on economic concerns. Atheism has given us the perception that we are what we own instead of owning what we are. Spirituality approaches life in the exact opposite direction—we are what we are, and what we own materially is very secondary. Our emergent Church, instead of instilling fear and insecurity, must become prophetic in its proclamation that we become most free when, by the subtraction of our material egotistical reality, we gain the wisdom of insecurity. Our emergent Church must walk and talk this message. It must be a promise more than a threat to a people already burdened down with too much negativity. It much be a Church that interpenetrates and imbues the secular with the spiritual. The emergent Church should have less and be more. Its gospel should be found in the ordinary experience of our everyday lives. The now here must connect with the nowhere. Heaven starts where the footfalls. Our future Church cannot be dualistic. Our future theology must be an applied and interpenetrating theism. It must be interfaced with even the smallest of our transactions, not only in our families but with the reality outside of us. Mystics are born in the small environment of our kitchens. There is no separation in spirituality. God is in our lovemaking and in the miraculous interior cleansing of our bodies through the ordinary working of our kidneys. Our pain is even a blessing. It is an alarm clock which sends out a siren to pay attention to a malfunctioning part of our bodies.

To be spiritual is to know that our eating of green spinach and lettuce will connect us to green pastures of sustenance. I shall not want. I will see diamonds hanging on the wet grass, but I will not be urged to grasp them. I will linger awhile to appreciate them and notice their tenuousness and fragility. There is a whisper and then disappearance. There is an invisible urgency running through everything. We colour the flowers and the green dollops of spring with our attitude. What is essential cannot be bought in department stores. What is essential costs nothing but our appreciation and attention. Parents must be the invisible spirituality they teach their children. Love is caught; it is not taught. A family is born out of spirituality rather than blood. There are connections in every reality. As the state operates honestly, so truth will be rampant in any society. A mustard seed explodes into a big bush. A watermelon is full with ten thousand seeds within it. Each one of has a mission with all kinds of possibilities inside of us. It is up to each one of us to reach our own possibility. It is our spirituality which will guide us. It is the invisibility of our interior which determines our exterior. Our environment determines our behaviour. When we live in a matrix of madness, we ourselves become mad from the anxiety and pressure imposed on us. When we live in a spiritual matrix, then all life lives in inter-relationship, interconnection, and interdependence.

The Cosmic Christ

> I see his blood upon the rose
> and in the stars the glory of his eyes.
> His body gleans amid eternal snows

his tears fall from the skies …
all pathways by his feet are worn
his strong heart stirs the ever beating seas
his crown of thorns is twined in every thorn
his cross is every tree
—Joseph Mary Plunkett

Love God's creation
love every atom of it separately
and love it also as a whole;
love every green leaf
every ray of God's light
love the animals and the plants
and love every inanimate obstacle.
If you come to love all things
you will perceive God's mystery inherent in all things,
once you have perceived it
you will understand better and better every day.
And finally you will love the whole world
with a total universal love
—Fyodor Dostoevsky

everybody is responsible for every one else
but I am more responsible for every body else than anybody else
—Fyodor Dostoevsky

It is here in the midst of the ordinary, perplexed, confused, struggling, psychologically damaged human society that an emergent Church must hammer out its compassionate narrative. The invisibility of our spirituality must be actualised, or else it will be never known. A spirituality of consciousness is the compassion within each one of us. An emergent theology must be grounded on the anvil of the New Testament, but the hammering, painful and uncomfortable though it may be through hermeneutics, will render the truth behind the literal. An emergent Church must adhere to the truth of hermeneutics rather than the details. An emergent Church must face up to the crucible of doubt and adapt it to the ordinary, sometimes painful reality of life. The promise of eternal consciousness is ultimately our only consolation in a world stricken by terror. Life is filled with the unknown, just as it is with the known. If we perceive it, the known gives us faith, and the unknown gives us hope. In the midst of our pain, an unknown hope is better than doubt. Compassion teaches us this. The emergent Church must be humble and honest. It cannot be imperial, declaring it alone has all the answers. It is only through a struggle for meaning that revelation lifts us up to a higher level of understanding. An emergent Church must again connect with the findings of legitimate science gives to us. An emergent theology must weave the strands of its own revelation and connect them to the same basket as the strands of scientific revelation. In the emergent Church, heaven will not be separated from earth nor the body from the soul. All life will be considered sacred, each according to its strand of electromagnetic specificity connected together. The prayers of our new Church will arise from the muck and pain of our ground, the stars in our black skies, the speech of our hedges, and the robins' nests within them. Perhaps our new prayers will ask us to kiss a tree rather than say a Hail Mary. Priests will be replaced by poets and mystics. The mitres of bishops will be replaced by the caps of farmers. Popes will be respected for their wisdom, imagination, and intuition rather than for their dogmas. Stories told from an older tradition will remain pregnant with wisdom in them, but they will be retold and adapted in a new way according to the language of the contemporary. The emergent Church, disenchanted by the past, will re-enchant itself and connect with the joy and the sorrow of everyday living. It will walk compassionately behind every hearse in a funeral procession and give a sense of communal belonging to people in their grieving may feel desperately lonely.

James Joyce said very prophetically, "God is a cry in the street." This insight from one of the world's greatest writers is at the heart of what our emergent Church must be. Organised religion has failed to address the cries of the street. Caught up in its own fanciful theology, it has failed miserably in its mission to interpenetrate and apply the counterculture teachings of Jesus to a world desacralised by atheism. When we live only on the level of the material, all the passion for the eternal becomes depleted. Atheism destroys our possibilities But as Joyce said, "It is far better to pass into that other world with some great passion than to fade and die dismally with age." Great literature is always truthful. It is intuitive and imaginative. It symbolically connects the present with a more transcendent future. Great literature is basically spiritual. It enlarges. Atheism can be challenging but never conclusive. Objectivity is not possible without subjectivity. The human person is always participatory in any scientific experiment. There can be no truth without imagination and intuition. To leave oneself open to higher possibilities as quantum physics demands is far more sensible and coherent than the certitude which atheism offers. Poets and mystics who enter this mystery make an ecstatic connection between finiteness and infinity.

Revelation is ongoing. The ineffable mystery of God is inexhaustible. As life unfolds, we are presented with new challenges and questions. Truth requires an antecedent refinement. The honest man is the one he knows very little. The mystic is never conclusive or haughty. To know is also to unknow. An emergent Church must be an hermeneutical Church—a Church in search rather than a Church of dogmas and sure answers. An emergent Church must walk with a confused people whose moral compass has been stolen from them. An emergent Church must, through its theology, raise the human imagination to a higher level. It must dismiss the agenda which had hitherto kept its faithful on a sixth-grade level of education. Instead of credal prayers, novenas, and dualistic devotions, a new and emergent Church must connect the outside to the inside; matter, though passing, is holy. The universe can be found in a grain of sand. The most exquisite stained-glass windows display their beauty in the midst of the ordinary. The world of nature is original. All human creativity is a copy. Just as our great music, paintings, and poetry erupt invisibly from the spirit of man, so also the natural world erupts from a presence of intangible and invisible beauty. Who chooses the colour and amazing design in the flower? Who paints them? How does the soil know how to prepare the precise chemicals to produce a specific colour.? Who puts the green into the teal's feathers? There seems to be an unseen intelligence behind all created beauty. If we were not so misinstructed, like John Donne we would see

> the world in a grain of sand
> and heaven in a wild flower.
> Hold infinity in the palm of our hand
> and eternity in an hour.

We are parts of a whole. We are connected and exist within the whole. If, together with the whole, we were to use the randomness of inversion imposed on us and turn the iceberg of atheism upside down, then its grip on our perception would surely drown. It is only through this overthrow that peace will reign on earth. No matter how atheism has controlled our perception, the fact remains that death shatters our horizontal materialistic illusions.

Our emergent Church will be a Church of feeling and emotions rather than rational and analytical. A Church which is all head and no heart is as irrelevant and destructive to the future of our world as the robotic AI utopia promised by smart technocracy. A Church which lives only on the conscious rational level has little imagination. The emergent Church will live on the intuitive unconscious level. An emergent Church will challenge us to get out of the bottle of our own ego and connect with the struggles wonders and perplexities outside of itself. An emergent Church will respect the feminine and the masculine inside each of us. The aggressive and dominant aspect of the male will be in balance with the intuitive, sympathetic aspect of the female. An emergent Church will be an "animamus" An emergent Church will create harmony between man and nature. An emergent Church will recognise a vitalising, penetrating power in all sentient being. Consciousness envelops all that exists. It is the bottom and the top, the inside and the outside of all that exists. Quantum teaches the world that the sacred and the eternal do exist. We all live in a cosmic unity. An emergent Church will be compelled to challenge to face a culture with no purpose or meaning to it. The God of the emergent Church will not be dualistic but will be a transcendent reality living in immanence. God is in this world already.

Christianity is an Eastern religion. Because of the dualism of organised religion, the Western church strayed from its Eastern origin. It separated itself from the real world. The emergent church unites all with a cosmic vision. God is in the water, the fire, the plants and the trees. God is accessible and touchable. Our perception makes divinity available. God is the ultimate experience of the soul. We live anthropologically, and for this we are limited. It is very difficult for Western people to understand that invisibility defines what is most real about us. We ourselves are cosmotheandric. There is external world outside of us. All life is permeated by God. The West vests its belief system on mathematics, and we believe it is "true", but it is a very abstract and cold language. Real truth, however, can be found only through imagination and intuition, which is beyond all language. God is an experience. The language of the Bible and the language of the poets is full of symbolism. Apart from this symbolic language, we can never attempt to define the ineffable God. God is our incommunicable search for the incomprehensible. God is the archetypal uncreated creator of the universe. All of our seeing, hearing, and knowing comes from the perceptions that we ourselves are participators in the one consciousness of the God who created us.

No matter what atheism throws at us, we must trust love above everything. Love is the only energy which will mend the broken vessel of our human existence. Love is stronger than even death itself. If atheism believes it is progressive, then surely it is an oxymoron. How can a system which declares itself to be progressive reconcile itself with its own claim that life is a mere chance without meaning or purpose? Has Godot gone, or are we still waiting for him?

Samuel Becket's play *Waiting for Godot* is a masterpiece. Perhaps more than any other play it summates the theatre of the absurd. But just as surely as truth is formed through a combination of the known and the unknown, life is as likely to be meaningful as the meaninglessness which Samuel Becket offers.

Even if we remain sceptical, we should remain open to the possibility of new revelation.

"Faith Comes Through a Crucible of Doubt"
—Fyodor Dostoevsky

An emergent Church, rather than giving dogmatic and irrelevant teachings which organised religion has imposed on society, must concern itself as much with doubt as it does with faith. An emergent Church must hammer out its faith on the anvil of its own humility and doubt. An emerging Church must reimagine God. It must say adieu to the old God of duality and place divinity right in the middle of struggling humanity. All creation, no matter the level of its consciousness, exists in and through the same bedrock of unity. Atheism has dismissed the vertical in our critical engagements.

The emerging Church will be non-dual. It will be a Church of unity where immanence connects with transcendence, where the body is holy and the vessel carries the human spirit into its fullest expression. Jesus represents the coming of God and the human together. He said, "I have come to take you with me." Life is more than little me. To be spiritual is to know that I am about life. A bigger reality enfolds me. Life is a dance between the self and the false self. The emergent Church will be a prayer much more than saying credal prayers. It is those behind the prayer who bring glory to God. Prayer can be a big lie when you are forced to say it, simply because it is not free. Prayer must erupt from the human heart. It is a cry and conversation much more than the rote recitation of a rosary. If we do not know how to be present to a presence, we cannot meditate or contemplate. When we are on the edge of losing life, perhaps for the first time we begin to appreciate its beauty and tranquillity. A virus which incarcerates us can be the very catalyst which teaches us the internal meaning of freedom. The now of our reality is all-important. We are already spiritual. We are already connected to our ultimate essence. How we live in the now impacts on our connection or separation from the God of our consciousness. To experience life on a surfaced, logical, linear way is not enough. We have to transfer from the little self into the larger self. All death is a transference of attention. When we realise our spiritual dimension then death has no more power over us. Death is actually a freeing experience. Because death is a taboo in our modern atheistic world, we think of it as something morbid. It terrifies us. The atheistic new world order has monopolised on our innate fear of death in order to control us and initiate their final plan to genocide most of us. Life is much more lateral than linear. It is both vertical and horizontal.

Spirituality will instruct us how to get rid of the mental grid with which atheism has anesthetised and calcified us. It will teach us how to process from the manifest into the unmanifest. To find God, we must seek him in his simplest, immediate form. We meet him in the midst of our everyday chores, our sacrifices, and our attentions. Teenagers who challenge their parents with a growing sense of their own individuality and individuation can be very difficult to manage. In their deepest souls, they are looking for love and attention, but they do not know it. If parents do not present them with limits, teenagers will register this as a rejection and lack of attention in their later lives. A parent-child relationship is the most fragile connection in this world. If parents do not waste themselves with the seed of a difficult love, then there will be chaff instead of kernels on the heads of the autumn offerings. God is found simply in the ordinary relationship between parents and their children.

The emergent Church must be to the forefront in removing prayer from a church sanctuary and reposting it in the midst of the ordinary. We remain unfocused souls when we have not learned the power of own interiority. A body separated from the human mind destroys our connection to the divine. It is non-holographic. Atheism teaches the separation of the actual self from the idealised self. It dwells on the little self rather than the higher self.

In our emergent Church, God will be approached not as an imperial dictator at the top but as one who walks amongst us in all our shortcomings and incompleteness. God will be our original ground who supports us as a cornerstone supports its edifice. Jesus taught us this. He sacrificed his life by his witness to the hopeless and the weary. He showed compassion to the prostitutes and the lepers. The few Christians who have followed his way have brought more inspiration to this world than all of our governments joined together.

The Emerging

The Church will respect Jesus as the great eschatological icon. He will always remain the way, the truth, and the life. He will always be the one, the true, and the beautiful. Islam, one of the monotheistic religions, claims there is only one God and respects Jesus as a great prophet. In the emergent Church, God will be God no matter what. As Hinduism says, "Thou are that", with this understanding Christianity can learn to move from the head into a heart-based theology. We are in each other, and God is within each one of us. Quantum physics is not partial. We live in a nest of unity. The geoengineering of the atheist squad incorporates a far different agenda. It seeks a one-world economy and a one-world religion to manage and control us. Through its self-image of supremacy, it plans to transpose our spiritual sovereignty into a state of submission and slavery.

The new normal is now enfolding We live in a new economic system where our over-commercialised consumer system which has dominated our perception is already in its death throes. The incremental inversion of the new world order is already casting its net of entrapment around our bodies. The old economy of paper money is about to be replaced by a digitalised version in a cashless society. The atheistic rich few are well on their way to committing genocide on most of the human race. They consider us useless. Their coronavirus is but a rehearsal for Armageddon. When perceived on the level of the irreducible, the coronavirus is used to keep humanity on the level of natural selection. In evolutionary terms, atheism locates us on the animal level without a soul the atheism of the new world order denies process into a higher realm.

Economy is central in its control mechanism. Through the coronavirus, this elite cult of death has distracted and denied us our spiritual identity. It has crucified our holographic reality. We have allowed this to happen because of our passiveness.

This elite death cult cannot ultimately succeed in its mission of genocide simply because the paradox of polarity is innate in all reality. Evil is destructive, but it is necessary so that good can overcome it. A greater good always arises when it is tested by its opposite. Our cosmos, by its very nature, is unitive. Our consciousness determines our faithfulness to what is most noble and holographic about us. Consciousness cannot be pre-empted. Consciousness is the law of all that is natural. What is eternal cannot ever be destroyed by the temporal. The very process of genocide which the new world death cult envisions for us can in fact become the very instrument which will awaken us to the holographic dimension of our existence. The elite of our world, who own 98 per cent of its wealth, wish to eliminate us so that they may inherit a pristine environment. They are using the covert instrumentation of the coronavirus to accomplish their mission. However, the plans of puny, evil men can never remove what is eternal from the temporal. Paradoxically, the separation which the coronavirus is imposing on human society is the very catalyst for our concern for one another. Just as the human family has an innate fear of death, so also has it an innate sense of community for preservation. We recognise our inseparateness. We begin to realise our spiritual dimension. From our inner core, without ever articulating it, we know deeply that indeed, yes, we are our brother's and sister's keeper, or as the Hindus say, "Thou art that." Fathers and mothers join more intimately and recognise far more deeply the precious fragility of their relationship with their children. The separation from the economy which the 2 per cent death cult envisions for evil purposes has in fact invited our eternal and internal values out of us. What is meant to suppress us has actually made us more resilient and enthusiastic. For the first time in our contemporary atheistic paradigm, we have begun to appreciate our own inner resources. The diabolic system cannot conquer us when we awaken from the slumber of our passiveness. If the atheistic death cult can terrify us through the invisibility of the coronavirus, then as spiritually awakened individuals, we can coax this world into a more holographic perspective. Atheism has brought us to the cliff's edge, but our spirituality gives us wings to fly. Through a sense of the higher self, we can lift our tired eyes beyond the trivial and recognise we are heirs to a kingdom that is eternal. The atheistic death cult of the new world order has already blinded us too much. Their incremental and covert plan to destroy us cannot eliminate the presence of the divine in the paradox of our human existence. Our spirituality will make us see a new heaven and a new earth everywhere.

> Shall I take the rainbow out of the sky
> and the moon from the well in the lane
> and break them in pieces to coax your eye
> to slumber a while again?

> When you know yourselves
> then you will know you are
> children of the living father
> —Gospel of Thomas

> If you do not know yourselves
> then you will die in poverty
> and it is you who are that poverty
> —Gospel of Thomas 3

> I emerge from the mind's care
> into a worse darkness outside where things pass
> and the Lord is in none of them.
> I have heard the still small voice
> and it was that of the bacteria demolishing my cosmos.

I have lingered too long on this threshold
but where can I go?
To look back is to lose the soul
To look forward. AH!
What balance is needed at the edge of such an abyss!
I am alone on the surface of a turning planet.
What to do but like Michelangelo's Adam
put my hand out into unknown space
hoping for the reciprocating touch
—R. S. Thomas

The coronavirus issued by the death cult may indeed be the very seed for a new beginning. As Jesus told us in the Gospel of Thomas, poverty exists within us. An external poverty caused by the economic collapse of a death squad cannot be the final blow to our peace and happiness. We have already been over-controlled in our present experience of economic control. It has already overwhelmed us with stress, anxiety, and madness. The natural inclination of parents is to protect and guide their children. The natural instinct of community living is to gather in celebration, kick off their shoes, and feel free enough to dance and sing in a martigra of festivity. With or without the coronavirus's attempt to herd us like sheep to the slaughterhouse, the time had already been ripe to overthrow the control and power which the 2 per cent death cult has imposed on us through economics. Our belief in a higher power is the only reality which will save us. Instead of separating and dividing us, the coronavirus can provide us with a time for meditation and contemplation about our holographic reality. The death warrant sent out by the atheist death cult may, through their economic control, incarcerate our bodies, but they cannot steal our souls. When we look out on the world of nature, birds are singing, and cats are having kittens. Day follows night in faithfulness, cows are lowing in the fields, dogs are still barking, flowers are still blooming, bees are still pollinating, and nature carries on with its own frequency. No strand strays into another's company except for humans.

Profit and economy have divided us and ruined the frequency upon which a supreme artificer has placed us. The purpose of life is to stay on the band which the ineffable God has platformed us. Try as we may, we will always live with an unquenchable longing when we remain on the material, economical level. The terror which the coronavirus engenders can be a blessing in disguise if we allow it to transfix our attention on what is primary rather than what is trivial. The task before us now is to spiritualise. This is the only way we can puncture the new world order. Our present system of economics will, because of the coronavirus, shatter the shell of our present security. But through this painful experience, it can also catapult us into a deeper appreciation of our holographic immanence and transcendence. Through isolation, we can teach our children how to cook. We can give them our time instead of our money. We can introduce them to the lost art of knitting, We can read the Bible or decipher for them some of the hidden messages in great literature. Instead of the virtual world of our smart televisions, we can expose them to the real and transient messages of the natural world.

In our rediscovery of the sacred and the divine, we will convert to the ordinary. Instead of fighting, we will associate with each other and recognise our unified ground of being. Already the skies look more blue, devoid of the pollution which the commercialism of the economy has caused. A blanket of greatness and newness will cover our planet if we change our perspective from the sensate into the state of the invisible, infinite possibility which consciousness offers.

The coronavirus has been dumped on us by the elite death cult as a rehearsal run for our final elimination. This group of death agents have always considered the rest of humanity as inferior, as apart from their own club. Rich elites have held the human race in slavery and low-level consciousness. We have been stuck with a low false self. Contrary to the very intent of the coronavirus, we, the 98 per cent of the human race, can use its very intrusion by damning and drowning its intention. We can use its stimulation contrarily and change our perspective towards a higher self. We can take a step out of the economic reality which has controlled us and move from its darkness into a much more enlightened world with God at its centre. Because of injustice, the coronavirus can become the very stimulant for a spiritual new world order.

We can learn how to pray again and connect with God, who exists in our feeding and eating, our lovemaking and human differences, our washing of clothes and dishes—all that is ordinary and simple. The contemplative mind connects and inserts the divine infinite in the simplest chores and the humility of service. There is a cosmic allurement and enchantment between all living things which stand on their own platform of electromagnetic wavelengths.

Atheism has twisted this blessing and, for the sake of economy and profit, has weaponised it through its smart technology. It has used the coronavirus to abuse us and control us. The coronavirus is in every one of us to a larger or lesser degree. But the new world order uses the detection of it within our DNA to terrify us with the immediate threat of death unless we isolate and obey its orders. The coronavirus is used deceptively to collapse our present economy. It signifies a lethal plan for the destruction of our humanity. It will push us further into a cashless society where the digitalised grid of control will take away all human rights from us. We will be forced to live on a universal wage system of austerity, which will scarcely sustain us. The coronavirus is in everyone, we battle with it all the time through our immune systems. If we really understand its complexity in itself, it is a marvellous invitation to the cells in our bodies to produce billions of antigens to fight off its intrusion. Its presence is part of the paradox of opposites. Essentially, it is another instance of the dark battling with light. Coronavirus is sickness fighting wellness. The death cult of the new world order has posted the coronavirus as some kind of a strange, newly mutated attack called COVID-19, which, we are told, will kill us because our cells have not learned how to fight it. The fact remains, however, that the coronavirus which already exists inside of each one of us, rather than its mythical COVID-19 component, is what is killing the most vulnerable amongst us. It is mostly those whose immune systems are already compromised that the coronavirus targets.

The fear with which the death cult of the new world order has duped us is a psy-ops. It is a shutdown of our freedom of movement. It is all about a creeping control and a delegitimisation of our dignity and spirituality. Even our churches and places of worship have been forced to shut down by the hoax of the coronavirus. The whole purpose of the coronavirus scare is to separate the vast majority of the human race from one another. The coronavirus is but the latest incremental, covert device which adds to the digitalised apps that are intended to separate and divide us communally. Our smart internet and our notorious preoccupation with smartphone technology serve to separate us from the real. More and more we live virtually instead of naturally. We like the milk, but we forget the cow. The intention of the 2 per cent rich cult that controls us economically is to destroy us spiritually. This notorious cabal of psychopaths have no belief in our human holography. Their whole aim is to totally destroy body and soul together. The only possible solution to this system of impalement is through the awakening of our God-given consciousness. Because the divine is in every aspect of our humanity, it is our own resilience which can combat the evil of a global economy. It is through our reacquaintance with the earth and its soil that we can find the nourishment to sustain us. It is through bartering and the rediscovery of human skills that we can bring balance back into our lives. Bartering and skills, instead of handing ourselves over to the control of global corporations, is what we need now most of all. Our hearts must again enter our workforce. We become depressed and feel useless when our spirituality is hammered out of us. While we can, before Armageddon descends totally upon us, we must again bless the birds and the bees and realise that onions, carrots, parsnips, cabbage, milk, and water are full of more blessings than the internet of things and smart technology can ever offer us. A horse has more power within itself than in all the technology of motor cars. Technology can give us speed, but it will never feed us. Technology is virtual, but life is real. Life comes from the heart rather than steel. Nutritious bread will never harm us, but the virtual world of technology can destroy us if we do not use it carefully.

We can, through our spirituality, denounce the whole matrix of moral destruction and chaos in our present culture. The truth of our decadence is adequately demonstrated by statistics. Life has become so purposeless that forty-five thousand Americans commit suicide every year, and seventy-two thousand live on opiates to escape a meaningless existence. Our new normal must be spiritual if we are not to succumb to more lethal attacks which the likes of the coronavirus has already visited upon us. Our worst mistakes have the seed within them to give us the best answers. As St Iraneus said, "God's glory is man fully alive." Our spirituality is not anti-fun. It does not weigh a tonne. It is as light as light. It enlivens us. It enlightens us.

The coronavirus has terrified us simply because of our innate fear of death. Even though we pay little attention to the inevitability of death's onslaught and progress, we know it finally demolishes all our gains in worldly possessions. In its essence, death is much more about detachment than attachment to material possessions. Atheism concerns itself with the present to the detriment of the hereafter. Yet as we have contemplated in this book, there are billions of incidents in this world which show the presence rather than the absence of some great non-local intelligence behind the mechanics of our planet.

Atheism may be imperial, but it is not empirical.

Atheistic values may come and go, but they are never stable. Humanity's search for God has always persisted throughout the ages. There has always remained in the human mind an ache for significance and meaning. The atheism of our present matrix is unique in its appearance. No people before us have ever been so outlandish in its dismissal of some higher being. Our present matrix dismisses all the wisdom of the ages. It has become so impertinent and arrogant that it has taken the sceptre from the godhead and placed it, like Napoleon, on the head of its own intelligence. Communism and fascism, which are the symptomatic cause of all our dishevelment and chaos, emphatically wish to destroy religion—perhaps even justifiably. But all the cruelty which the enactment of their vision causes can never destroy our innate spirituality. Essentially, we are spiritual beings with only a time-bound materiality. No matter the crucifixion of the human body, our eternal consciousness continues. No matter the progress we may have accomplished through our AI and smart technology, it can never change one iota of our spiritual identity. Holographically, we remain now as we ever were and ever will be in eternal consciousness. This is our history since the Big Bang of God's interiority,

We may pride ourselves about our modernity, technological achievements, and the awesome power of our war defence system, but because physical death is our only promise, why the hell are we always on the prowl to destroy one another? Death can be a deterrent to slaughter instead of its opposite. Death changes all our perceptions when we recognise its spiritual message. It can blind us or amend us. No matter our perspective, the reality of death cannot be swept under the carpet by Silicon Valley and the rich at Davos. The real problem with our planet is that we, the impoverished citizens, have not awakened to the divine gift of consciousness, and the 2 per cent who possess all the wealth have totally dismissed God as of no consequence.

When we live on the spiritual level, we live more sustainably and simply. We connect mystically with the interior messages which the ordinary natural world speaks to us. God becomes our comfort and our solace. The pain, the death, and the sorrow are turned into acceptance. "Welcome be the holy will of God." Our modern world thinks of such resignation as pure madness. But in ultimate terms, like it or not, we all must accept and surrender. Death is the great equaliser. No matter how we cover it up with our lipstick and powder, the body will one day fall into dust, and no power on earth can cover it up. Death is a morbid reality to those who have a morbid mentality, but to a people of faith, disease becomes a release into a God who, through the dominion of consciousness, eases all our pain and diseases.

A Meditation on Death

"I saw my son … I saw my son in the picture of that little boy you showed on the screen. I saw my son. He looked out at me as plain as day on the movie screen. Oh, God, my only son! Why did he have to disappear and go from me in such a horrible way? Why did he have to leave his father and me on that God-forsaken day? It's over … it's all gone … Tell the sun to stop its light. It's all a cod. Night is the only truth! The rest's a lie! Life will never be the same again. The Grand Canyon is little in comparison to the deep hole in my heart.

"Stop all the bloody singing and laughing! How can anyone laugh again? Doesn't everyone know this world has come to a standstill? The impudence of those birds to go on flying in the sky! Why aren't they roosting in a requiem? The empty chatter from the television, radios, and ramblings of nothingness are an insult to my ears! Has this world forgotten the meaning of reverence and respect at this time of mourning? There was so much nurturing left undone. I could have cuddled him for a long time yet. Just a few short years ago, I suckled him. I could see even then he had the makings of a fine man. But why did it have to turn out this way? It's all a bloody mess! I still see the stain on the ground … Catapulted through the car window … That's how my darling son died. I thought he was buckled in, but for some reason he wasn't. Sometimes I feel I'm going insane. I can't forgive myself … Was it my negligence? If only I was given one more chance to check again!

"Maybe I didn't see his face on the movie screen … Maybe I'm going mad after all. Why did he have to die in such a dreadful way He had still so much in store for him. Why didn't God take me instead? I have lived. I have tossed my hair through the long fingers of the sun and splashed in the puddles on the lane. He was just beginning. Four years old was all he was. There were still so many gates for him to climb over, or to find bird's nests in the ditches. His hair was curly gold like the barley fields in autumn … Oh, God, that gold. I'd give my legs, my ears, my tongue, my taste, my smell, my right hand just to run the fingers of my left hand through his curly golden hair once again. He knew the Father and me loved him through and through. That much we know. We have no regrets in that respect. Love is all that matters. That is our only recompense. He was the Sunday in our week, but that Sunday is only a nightmare now that he is gone. The bloody crash … his poor little head and broken back. God, where were you when my only son was taken from us? I used to believe in you, but now I am not so sure."

To shake one's fist at God at a time like this is indeed a rational prayer. Life is unfair at times. There are no quick solutions or easy answers to the searing pain of those who are grieving for the premature death of a child. Easy cliches and stopgap theological answers add insult to injury at times of such intense distress. There is a presence in silence, and our best prayer is to say nothing. It is our presence which says everything. The silence of presence is our unspoken language of comfort and connection. The cry of Job has is still the painful cry of the human heart for validation. It cannot be resolved in terms of what our present world has to offer. It is easy to believe in God when we have no reason to deny his animamus. It is easy to be courageous when we have no reason to feel afraid. To believe is to question. Faith is doubt negotiated. Theism and agnosticism are strange bedfellows. If we lived in a world of easy grace, bereft of pain and suffering, we would live on a stage of puppets, manoeuvred by a controlling marionettist. We would live as nicely behaved zombies and robotised entities, bereft of spontaneity, flexibility, freedom, and love. Our world would be a drab place.

Paradoxically, it is suffering and a death to self which gives us life and love. We become our own best versions and find our greatest peace within ourselves when we sacrifice ourselves for the sake of others. Spirituality is meant by nature to be our only economy. Mystical theology teaches that when the visibility of quantum ends, it transcends into new possibilities of consciousness. Light becomes pure and more translucent when we reach the most irreducible particle of matter. The timeless awaits us when the material expires. Death is our threshold into a placeless timelessness. Death is a transmutation more than a transformation. In respect to suffering and death, evolution will not barter with us. There is no compromise. Death is the only expert. We can choose to fight suffering and death. To refuse the natural process will forever make us outcasts. Death is the only tribalism and separation which nature finds acceptable. Just as yeast ferments sourdough to make a loaf of bread, so too do we need the disturbance of suffering to swell ourselves into a more sacred offering. Discontent is a longing for something better and greater than what the present offers. Our hearts remain restless until they rest in God. Suffering instructs us. Discontent can be the very instrument for a greater discovery and enlightenment. We are doomed to be spiritual We have no choice but to go for the ride. We can despair, but that is akin to throwing ourselves off a speeding train. The overwhelming insights from our cosmological and mysterious world give us a new perspective on the meaning of suffering and death. Job did not know, and neither did Darwin, that evolution is a soul-making machine. Neither of them understood that evolution supports our homographic explanation as unitive much more than it does the dualism which separates the body from the soul. The New Testament teaches, "Jesus learned obedience through suffering."

> God whispers to us in our pleasures
> speaks in our conscience
> but shouts in our pain
> It is his megaphone to rouse a deaf world
> —C. S. Lewis

We become too consumed with the short-range experiences of suffering and death but fail to recognise the eternity of harmony coming out of chaos. We want the smell of the summer flower but not the patience of the shivering shoot in the grip of winter. Grief has its own schedule. First there must be recognition and reflection, then commemoration, and then reorientation.

As the Irish poet Conrad Aiken wrote,

> Music I hear with you was more than music,
> and bread I broke with you was more than bread:
> Now that I am without you, all is desolate
> all that was once so beautiful is dead
> Your hands once touched this table and this silver,
> and I have seen your fingers hold this glass.
> These things do not remember you beloved
> and yet your touch upon them will not pass.
> For it was in my heart you moved among them
> and blessed them with your hands and eyes
> and in my heart they will remember always—
> they knew you once, oh beautiful and wise
>
> Day by day, hour by hour
> pain drops upon the human heart against our will
> and in spite of it comes wisdom
> from the awful grace of God
> —Aeschylus

Having reached the bottom, the grieving person finally realises all portals have been closed except in one small shaft of unfamiliar light. The obsessiveness of depression and anxiety begins to shake. Often revelation comes not through earthquakes but in the shivers and whispers which creep in through the cracks of our broken hearts.

Samuel Beckett, one of Ireland's best-known writers, paints a bleak picture about human existence when he declares, "Every time I go out into the world, it is suicide, but if I stay at home, it is slow dissolution." When confronted by such desolation, we must of course respect this resolution. But we must also be allowed question it. Absurdity is negative by its very nature. It is not a reality which builds up creativity. There remain billion of clues from our world of phenomenology which indicate some invisible tremendous intelligence behind the structure of the universe. Indeed, the very genius of Beckett's mind is sourced by an energy that he declares does not exist. Creativity and creator are synonymous. Compassionate atheistic artists are reluctant at best.

When we look deeply into life, we see everything in this world is on loan to us. We arrived as babies without shirts to our names, and we will leave in the same way. We own nothing. We are owned. "Goodbye … God be with you … Adieu …" is the one inaudible, all-enveloping, and encompassing song of the cosmos. Whether or not we hear it, it sees and feels us. It approaches us daily without our permission or consent. It will not leave us alone. Like the waves on our shore, death is always waiving at us. Goodbye is the musical refrain of the universe. Life takes a breath, and then it blows it out again; there is no standing still. Death and resurrection, resuscitation and despoliation, coin here all the time. Oscillation like the swing of a pendulum is imperial. In and out, back and forth are the notes of the human symphony. Death and life, like man and wife, are the one reality. They ache for one another when either of them is absent. Life without death is a contradiction. Both are notes in the one melody. To avoid their presence in the midst of our distractions is to live timidly and terminally with life failure. As Ecclesiastes says,

> There is a season for everything
> a time to be born and a time to die
> A time for tears and a time for laughter
> a time for mourning and a time for dancing

The perishability, fragility, and changefulness of our aching world is part of its very liveliness and loveliness. Every leaf on the autumn tree is a tongue which tells us a story about our own autumn. Put all the coloured leaves together, and they speak as one.

There is a melancholy to our flow. We want to cry, "Not yet." But nature beckons more powerfully: "Be satisfied … Surrender … Let go." The wisdom of insecurity is all we need to know.

The leaves fall to the ground only to enrich the soil for another growth in another year. As Henry David Thoreau said, "Am I not partly leaves, vegetables and mould myself?"

The seasons are chat rooms of information speak to us of our own rhythm. If we live in the fields and the woods, God will speak to us every day. Even when we live in cities, we live in connection with the food that sustains us. We pray when we keep that dependency and relationship alive within us. Re-enchantment with the revelation of nature releases us from the morbidity of death. Like the leaves of autumn, from the moment of our birth, our going forth is a process into saying goodbye. Though we may not perceive it, nature works as much in our interior as it does on the outside. Nature is a consistent and truth-filled teacher, and it is the greatest foe to those who try to distract humanity from its evolutionary journey into a higher sphere.

Like the leaves of autumn, we all remain in the happenstance of our own leaf taking. We move from babyhood into childhood and the promise of security. We move from childhood into adolescence, individuation, and the assertion of our individualisation. We begin to experience confusing uncertainties and the rip-roaring fires of an awakening sexuality. We bond and get married only to beget beginners in the never-ending tremors of oscillation. A new generation begins in exactly the same place and time as we ourselves once existed, only to begin another circle of goodbyes.

Wrinkles, sagging skin, aching bones, and dimming eyes compel us to recognise that a force much larger than ourselves is urging us through decomposition into a deeper compensation and transformation. Only the little child and the old know what they are seeking.

> An aged man is but a paltry thing
> A tattered cloak upon a stick
> Unless soul clap his hands
> And sing and louder sing
> for every tatter in its mortal Dress
> —William Butler Yeats

Change and Decay Are All Around Us in Our Everyday Lives

Ninety-eight per cent of the atoms in our bodies were not there a year ago. Our present skeleton was not there three months ago. Our skin is all new every month. We replace our liver every six weeks. We form a new brain every year. Building blocks are taken out and replaced in our bodies without our awareness. Our bodies are 70 per cent water. The materiality of our bodies are always oscillating, but the same spirit which saturates us never changes.

That which departs from us is like the leaves leaving their limbs of security. It becomes married to the vapor between the earth and the sky. It appears in the tear of another eye. It is in the drop of the snow and the grip of the ice. It runs in the river and the tumble of the waterfalls. It sleeps in the eternal clouds which the sun's penetration transubstantiates into pouring rain. Our loved ones may seem gone, but in reality they now live eternally in the one consciousness which only our imagination and intuition can point towards in a knowing and not knowing way.

We cry over the deaths of our loved ones and keep living with the hope we will live with them again. We have yet to learn that the consciousness into which they have departed is the same one consciousness which surrounds our daily world of the ordinary. We can electromagnetically communicate with all people that we love, be it in heaven or on earth, with the same invisible energy which pervades the universe. No matter what the arrogant atheistic scientists are attempting to do through the manipulation of this all-pervasive eternal energy, their attempt is but a fart in the wind. God will never retreat from nature or finally allow it to be weaponised. If we would only change the paradigm of atheism into a new world which really respects the dignity of not only Homo sapiens but in our subspecies world, then the power and control of the 2 per cent elitist, rich atheistic world would soon topple.

Life is more than what it seems to our way of seeing. It appears tangible and touchable. To say nothing about the dualism with which the Church indoctrinated us, modern science has now given a double hammering to the atheism of materialism. The atom itself is more full of emptiness and invisibility than the smallest particle of matter, yet atheism manages to hold its empirical grip on the illusion that matter is solid. Modern science now points to the reality of a spiritual presence behind consciousness.

God is with us now. Our loved ones have found their home in this sea of consciousness. We can gather together with them in our woods and our gardens. God is our companion in all our work and undertakings. It is the same consciousness which pervades the universe electrifies and lives in me. All that is needed is to our change of perception. All that is needed for us poor mortals is to change the focus of our attention to the reality that the energy which exists in me is the one energy that exists in the universe. No matter the separation and isolation which our atheistic masters impose on us through their misuse of electromagnetic waves, God is far more inexhaustible in his dispensation of divine energy than the manipulation and weaponisation with which evil men intend to destroy us.

Revelation and inspiration lie in the spiritual realm of consciousness. Atheism never generates inspiration. It has no measure for melody. It pours liquid through a sieve and ends up with a sticky pool of glue on the floor. Atheism is the arch-enemy of mysticism. It does not understand the paradox of human life as contradiction. Jesus said, "For whoever wishes to save his life will lose it. But whoever loses his life for God's sake will save it.

A baby in a womb is constructed effortlessly and silently. An invisible intelligent artificer lays the bricks for another masterpiece that is unique and different, never before seen in human history. The complexity of this incredible feat staggers all human perception. The robot machinery which humans have created on the physical level is but a copy of the original. No matter the power of AI or the fascist batteries of hatcheries, smart technology will never succeed in manufacturing a neurologically connected real human being with a compassionate heart inside of it. The invisibility of our spirituality can never be replicated no matter the app or software. If this ever happened, then all that apples in Silicon Valley would turn into the forbidden fruit on the tree in the Garden of Eden.

The remarkable feat of a newborn baby is that it was carved out in darkness. It had no idea of what life was like outside the womb. Yet it continued on as if it knew what it was doing. Why did it construct eyes to see light when all it knew was darkness? Why did it create hands and legs when they never knew what ground to touch or stand on? Yet marvellously it went on with its artistry in some spirit of expectancy. Could it be a tomb is a womb, or a womb is a tomb for a higher destiny? There is a lot of darkness in our present existence\, and we struggle to get out of its entanglement. Metaphorically we are now in a tomb of darkness, ready to break out into that womb of intelligent consciousness.

God's will be done! Puny atheist man, beware. You dabble too much in a territory where you do not belong.

> the moving finger writes and having writ, moves on
> Nor all the piety or wit shall hire it back to cancel half a line
> Nor all thy tears wash out a word of it

We live penumbral lives, but we have the resilience within ourselves to recreate. We live in darkness and suffering with the unmanifest. But a sweater can emerge from a ball of knotted wool, and heaven can be found through a heaven of suffering.

A beautiful piece of glass with a blower's breath infused in it can emerge from the torture of a hot fire. A piece of clay with the skill of a potter can be turned into a jug to hold milk. God is in the potter's hands and the breath of the glass blower.

When we learn to see with the eyes of our spirituality, then

> The year's at the spring,
> and the day's at the morn,
> morning's at seven
> the lark's on the wing
> the snail's on the thorn.
> God's in his heaven
> and all's right with the world
> —Robert Browning

Irish Celtic Spirituality

We live in depressing times. For five centuries, Irish Celtic spirituality managed to bring a new hope and buoyancy to the darkness and madness of continental Europe. They set up powerful monasteries of asceticism throughout Europe, including St Gaul in Switzerland, Tours in France, and Bobbio in Italy. St Francis was inspired by their witness and asceticism. Due to political disagreements and jealousy, Irish monasticism gradually faded into Cistercianism. The ancient Irish Church through its spirituality gave to this world something which neither psychology nor psychiatry ever could. It created a spirituality called Anam Cara, which means soul friend. In essence, this led to the unveiling of one's soul to a monk, which later turned into confession. Like the East, Irish Celtic spirituality was non-dual. It was the only Church in Europe which was non-empirical. Authority was circular. It fused and blended its theology with the tangible world around it. It interpenetrated earth with the light and the life in heaven. Immanence was intimately connected to transcendence.

Irish Celtic spirituality created a unique marriage between the ordinary and the eternal. The megalithic stone circle imposed upon the cross of Christ. It hammered out its theology on the megalithic culture, which already existed before AD 432 when Patrick came to convert the Irish to Christianity. The Irish Church became very strong not by abolishing the megalithic culture but by adapting it to the message of Christianity. The Irish Church did not take its inspiration from the mathematical and analytical logic of continental Europe but found it instead through the contemplative approach of the desert fathers in Egypt. Irish Celtic spirituality is truly Eastern. Christianity itself is an Eastern spirituality which does not separate or divide the soul from the body. As the mystic Irish poet Patrick Kavanaugh says, "God is found in common statement."

The Irish Church, true to its own culture, built its theology on the themes of its ancient pagan mythology. For instance, the story of Cuchulainn stood tall, tied to a stone even though he was dead, with a spear in his hand to frighten the enemy. This myth was adapted by the Irish Church to teach its people to face death with courage. Faith and hope live on long after we are gone. The Celtic Irish Church was essentially more coptic than Roman. The ancient Irish Church considered this world sacred and understood all life as breathing with divine consciousness. The ancient Irish Church is the only Church in Europe where East and West meet in their theology. The Irish Celtic Church is the only Church where the Megalithic Secular Culture and the spiritual blend harmoniously without any trace of animosity. During this peaceful reign, the Irish monks created beautiful masterpieces in gold and silver, but most of all they created masterpieces such as the Book of Kells in their scriptoriums. These masterpieces ran round in never-ending connection imitating the unity of all creation with Christ in the centre. Irish Celtic spirituality found its expression in the outdoors surrounded by nature. The great cathedrals of Europe in early Irish Christianity were built in the human heart of love and mystical wonder.

Students from all over Europe came to study at their Christian universities, which were mostly made of wattles and clay. The monks kept the high literature of Greek and Rome alive during Europe's Dark Ages, and as Perigrini, they sailed out on small boats to re-Christianise Europe. The continent, schooled in objective science, was introduced by the early Irish monks to the perception that life is more symbolic than it is literal. The vertical spiritual life was reignited on the continent by the early Irish monks. They taught that if we learn to live beneath the surface of everyday life, we will find invisible resources to assist us. This made an amazing contribution to the civilisation of life. The early Irish monks brought good news to European nations burdened with plague and desolation. Their essential teaching was that we are mystical beings caught in a biosphere. This world cannot hold us. We are destined for a heavenly Eden. Hope is needed before healing. Suffering has meaning. The vertical breaks into the horizontal when we cry in pain. "Where are you God?" is the deepest cry of the human heart. What is the point to all this drudgery and monotony? "God, are you there?" This cry and these tears expose our deepest reality. Tears drag us away from our horizontal fabrications and preoccupations. These early monks taught the people to look vertically. Ancient Irish spirituality asks that we squeeze God into our human perception. Only then will we find meaning and purpose. See God in the before and the hereafter. Put away your swords.

I arise today
through the strength of heaven
light of the sun
radiance of the moon.
Splendor of fire
speed of lightening
swiftness of wind
depth of see
stability of earth
firmness of rock.
Christ in the heart of everyone who thinks of me
Christ in the mouth of every person who speaks to me.
Christ in every eye that sees me
Christ in every ear that hears me.
—Breastplate of St Patrick

Early Irish Christianity stresses the inner friendship between heaven and earth, body and spirit, underworld and overworld, visible world and invisible world. There is only a thin edge or veil between reality and the mystical. Wonder, imagination, and intuition play a big role in early Irish spirituality.

God is the beneath of the beyond, the above of the under. God invades and sparks our every breath of life. Our superlatives about his divine ineffability are mere understatements. God is touchable but illusive. Ancient Irish spirituality is penumbral. It speaks about the root as much as the tree. It relishes the light but also takes notice of the shadow. Celtic spirituality suggests God's presence. It lies in the land of twilight. It is more like candlelight. It gives us intimations and abhors neon light. It suggests more than it explains. It is subterranean and erupts from the unseen. God is in its holy wells. The early Irish Church gave love. The Roman Church gave law.

The Roman Empire never reached Ireland. Instead of abolishing paganism, Christianity built on it. It embraced nature and the netherworld. The Roman Church imprisoned God in its tabernacles, but the early Irish Church allowed God to run free to visit his people and live amongst them. Spirituality was not an heirloom to be kept in a safe. We live on the edge of the divine all the time. Even our simplest chores are interpenetrated with the divine.

God is considered very near in early Irish spirituality Prayers were formulated for every human activity. The early Irish Church did not discern where spirituality begins and ends. It assumed God was lovingly concerned in all human activity. The woman of the house started her day by splashing her face with three palms of water in the name of the Trinity.

> The palmful of the God of life
> the palmful of the Christ of love
> the palmful of the spirit of peace upon me

In the early Irish Church, there was no dualistic difference between the sacred and the secular.

> I make this bed
> in the name of the Father and of the Son and of the holy Spirit
> In the name of the night we were conceived
> In the name of the day we were born
> in the name of the day we were baptized
> in the name of each day, each night
> each angel in heaven
>
> God kindle thou my heart as I kindle my morning fire
> a flame of love to my neighbor
> to my foe, to my friend, to my kindred all.
> Oh Son of the loveliest Mary
> from the lowliest thing that liveth
> to the highest name of all
>
> A hundred glories to you bright God of heaven
> who gave us this food and the sense to eat it.
> Give mercy and glory to our souls
> and life without sin
> to ourselves and the poor

Come Mary and milk my cow
Come Bridget and encompass her
Come Columba
and twine thine arms around my cow.
Bless Oh God each teat
Bless Oh God each finger
Bless Thou each drop
that goes into my pitcher, Oh God

I lie down this night with God
And God lies down with me
I lie down this night with Christ
And Christ will lie down with me
I lie down this night with Spirit,
and the spirit will lie down with me.
God and the Christ and the Spirit
Be lying down with me

The early Celtic Church saw the earth as good and all life as a generous blessing.

Divine allurement fills the Universe
The moon calls out to the tides
streams, rivers. Oceans
hug the earth and run their course.
Mountains, hills and crests
paps of the earth mother's breasts.
Love springs from ancient earth
when harvest come from the `divine
Fertile seed bed of yearning
Grapes of love
blessed be my Beloved

Marriage broker make a match
marriage broker make me a match
fire of Triune Love
Let me move from one to three
I, you. She

Celtic spirituality breaks into the ordinary, daily, mundane, and earthy. It is very much a down-to-earth spirituality. Any moment and any work can become a time and a place to encounter God.

Patrick Kavanagh, a modern poet in the mystical Irish tradition, wrote,

God is in the bits and pieces of every day.
A kiss here
and a laugh again
and sometimes tears.
A pearl necklace
around the neck of poverty

The ancient spirituality of Ireland has a deep sense of enchantment with the beauty and the mystery of the natural world.

Perhaps the greatest symbol of Celtic spirituality is the Irish high cross. One of the most magnificent high crosses stands in the ruined Monastery of Monsterbois. It dates from the tenth century, and the symbols are powerful. From a distance, it looks like the general perception we have of any Celtic cross, but this cross is an original, and upon closer inspection, it reveals a marvellous imaginative and intuitive approach to the Gospel message. It is unitive. The paradox of polarity is blatantly clear in its carving. The clash of opposites immediately grabs our attention. The pagan megalithic Circle of Creation is placed upon the cross of Jesus Christ. Creation comes out of suffering. The big O of the cosmos intersects and connects with the message of love which Jesus lived throughout his ministry. Four beams of light break forth from the imposition of the circle on the cross as if to say light comes out of darkness. The cross may be dark, but light shines through the cosmos because of the compassion and love of this singular man. We see on the central panel an extraordinary sight of crucified Christ wearing a long tunic. Life and death are held together as one in this image. There is no dualism. Over this central figure, in the dominant top panel we see carved images of St Anthony of Egypt and St Paul of Thebes—again, an extraordinary sight. Early Irish Christianity was Eastern and not Roman. Ancient Irish Christianity believed in thin lines and thin spaces where mystery was always clashing with human experience. Life is a clash of opposites. The mystical mind knows this immediately. We are one head with two different faces. One cries tears of joy while the other pours the water of sorrow down his face. The Irish high cross brings the cosmos and redemption together. It tells us Creation is not enough—there is a higher sphere beyond the mind which evolution intends to take us. We must first detach from the shackles of the ego in order to reach our next plateau. That is what the symbolism on the high cross of Monsterbois teaches us. The cosmic Christ is waiting for us to make the next step in our evolutionary process.

Our present world is broken. Smart technology and artificial intelligence are on the verge of gouging the human heart out of us. It is terrifying what these butchering, elitist psychopaths are covertly attempting to exercise upon us. They hate us. The holy high cross of Monsterbois has many lessons to teach us which are as relevant today as they were to the Dark Ages on the European continent. Jesus of Nazareth has been the central figure in the development of Western civilisation, yet neither Brussels nor Washington pay any attention to his message. Their only concern is the economy. They are empty of empathy. Cyberspace will soon obliterate his name from the face of the earth as though his teachings are irrelevant. Yet billions of dollars spent by a cult of death to indoctrinate and genocide us can take the human spirit out of us. Their agenda is hopeless. One little panel on a tenth-century Irish high cross says it all. The remarkable thing about this panel is that the carving of the crucified Christ extends his hand and arm to the whole world, but his arm and hand are huge and totally disproportionate to the rest of his crucified body. "Come to me all you who labour and over burdened and I will refresh you' we cannot but fall on our knees. What love! What compassion! What benevolence … what silence … the lark tumbled down music … ah but then planes full of soldiers on their way to war left white trails in the blue sky."

The Irish high cross, with its symbolism, has real wisdom to convey to us. We humans, in our cosmos, stand precisely in the middle where the vertical and the horizontal intersect. We humans live as one on the same horizontal beam. To find redemption, however, we have been created to connect with the vertical. We have been created holographically. We find God through each other, and as Celtic spirituality so beautifully teaches, "God is but an inch and a half above the head of a man."

Printed in the United States
by Baker & Taylor Publisher Services